Aliteracy

A Conference Sponsored by the
American Enterprise Institute for Public Policy Research

Aliteracy
People Who Can Read But Won't

Edited by Nick Thimmesch

American Enterprise Institute for Public Policy Research
Washington and London

Library of Congress Cataloging in Publication Data
Main entry under title:

Aliteracy, people who can read but won't.

(AEI symposia ; 83C)
Proceedings of a conference held Sept. 20, 1982, in Washington, D.C.
1. Books and reading—United States—Congresses.
2. Literacy—United States—Congresses.   3. Decision-
making—Congresses.   I. Thimmesch, Nick.   II. American
Enterprise Institute for Public Policy Research.
III. Series.
Z1003.2.A43   1983   028'.9'0973   83-15579
ISBN 0-8447-2247-2

AEI Symposia 83C
3 5 7 9 10 8 6 4

Printed in the United States of America

Contents

Foreword

Thomas Jefferson and the Founding Fathers understood the importance of an educated citizenry to the success of a democracy. Indeed, a shared culture and literacy were prerequisites to the formation of our democratic nation and remain the foundation for its preservation. Because literacy was conscientiously pursued, it has become accepted today as the norm in the developed nations of the world, and universal education is heralded as a historical achievement of American public schools. In spite of such success, however, two major literacy problems exist in America today: functional illiteracy and aliteracy.

An estimated 25 million Americans cannot read well enough to negotiate the daily business of life; they are functional illiterates. They cannot read an insurance policy, deal with an employment application, or follow directions on electrical appliances or instructions for assembling a bicycle. In contrast, aliterates are people who can read but do not. They scan magazines by looking at the pictures, do not read beyond the headlines on the front page of the newspaper, and never read novels or poetry for the pleasure they may offer.

The problems of illiterates in modern developed nations are personally, socially, and economically devastating. Learning disabilities, poor instruction, or lack of opportunity may have created their problem; shame and embarrassment allow it to persist.

As difficult as the problems of the functionally illiterate may be, aliteracy may be the more dangerous problem because of its potential effects on the future of our nation. Aliteracy reflects a change in cultural values and a loss of skills, both of which threaten the processes of a free and democratic society.

Literacy has two critical functions in a pluralistic society. First, it knits a people together, giving them a common culture. Of equal importance, literacy provides people with the intellectual tools used to question, challenge, understand, disagree, and arrive at consensus. In short, it allows people to participate in an exchange of ideas. A democratic nation is weakened when fewer and fewer citizens can participate in such an exchange. Aliteracy leads inexorably to a two-tiered society: the knowledgeable elite and the masses. It makes a common culture illusory or impossible; it erodes the basis for effective decision making and participation in the democratic process.

The problem raised in this volume is not an academic one. Nor is it simply nostalgia for the written word. Rapid changes and developments in technology are hurtling our society in the direction of a new electronic age. Information will be easily "accessed." The possibility of knowing without understanding increases as the need to decipher, select, and draw implications and inferences disappears. As Townsend Hoopes, former president of the Association of American Publishers, suggests in a paper included in this volume, the nonreader, unexposed to the precision of the carefully chosen word and the painstakingly constructed sentence, may lose the ability to be critical, analytical, and precise. When such skills fall into disuse, the implications for participating in the decision-making process of a modern society can be far-reaching.

The American Enterprise Institute is dedicated to the principle that the vigorous competition of ideas is fundamental to a free society. Its activities reflect this dedication. Through research, conferences, seminars, and publications, AEI provides an arena for the pursuit of scholarly, nonpartisan research and for the examination of competing public policy arguments. The issues raised by the problem of aliteracy are at the foundation of AEI's commitment to the competition of ideas and are thus central to all of its activities.

WILLIAM J. BAROODY, JR.
President
American Enterprise Institute

Contributors

JOHN J. CAMPBELL is a professor of reading at Howard University. He has served as a consultant to many school systems, government agencies, and corporations. Coauthor of two textbooks on the teaching of reading, he has also published widely in professional journals.

JOHN Y. COLE is director of the Center for the Book in the Library of Congress. The center works with publishing, educational, and other organizations to promote an awareness of books and to stimulate the study of books and reading. Dr. Cole was educated at the University of Washington, Johns Hopkins University, and George Washington University.

SHIRLEY FOUTZ, a specialist in education, is now director of Educational Services for the Richmond (Virginia) Newspapers. She has worked with teachers and school administrators in the forty-seven school divisions in Central Virginia to encourage the use of newspapers as a teaching tool. She holds a master's degree in education from Virginia Commonwealth University and is a doctoral candidate at that institution.

LYNNE GRASZ is director of Communications of the CBS Broadcast Group. She is producer of the "Read More about It" program, a series of television presentations linked to specific books. She began her career in Nebraska, working in St. Louis and Detroit before coming to New York.

TOWNSEND HOOPES has been president of the Association of American Publishers since 1973. After graduating from Yale, he began his writing career at the *Buffalo Evening News*. In 1969, his work, *The Limits of Intervention*, received the overseas writers' prize as the best book on foreign policy. Mr. Hoopes also served as undersecretary of the air force, among other important posts in the Pentagon.

MARSHA LEVINE is an education consultant at the American Enterprise Institute in Education Policy Studies. She was a policy fellow at the U.S. Department of Education and has many years of experience in teacher education and in classroom teaching. She holds degrees from Barnard College,

Teachers College of Columbia University, and a doctorate from the University of Maryland.

VINCENT REED, former superintendent of the District of Columbia public schools and then assistant secretary for elementary and secondary education with the Department of Education, is now vice president for communications at the *Washington Post*. A graduate of West Virginia State College, he has dedicated his professional career to education.

KENT RHODES is president of the Magazine Publishers Association. He was born in Brooklyn and educated at Dartmouth. Beginning his career in the magazine industry with Time Incorporated, he worked for Time-Life and Fortune before coming to the *Reader's Digest* in 1944. There, he was elected president in 1975, becoming chairman in 1976. He now serves as chairman of the Reader's Digest Foundation.

NICK THIMMESCH has had a career of thirty years in both print and broadcast journalism and is now resident journalist at the American Enterprise Institute.

ROBERT M. WILSON is director of the Reading Center at the University of Maryland. Born in California, he was educated at the University of Pittsburgh. He has written several books on reading, including *Using Newspapers to Teach Reading Skills*, published by the American Newspapers Publishers Association.

Introduction

MARSHA LEVINE: By way of introducing the question before this conference, I would like to pose two seemingly paradoxical observations. First, while educators have traditionally concerned themselves with achieving universal literacy in the United States and have been remarkably successful in this effort, we have a growing concern that many people are in fact reading less and that, in some cases, they might not be reading at all. Second, a revolution in technology is having and will continue to have enormous impact on education, but at the same time that new technologies increase the level of literacy, they might undermine the practice of what they teach.

One more comment—on the goals of education. Teaching someone to read is imparting a skill, while encouraging and stimulating the pleasure of reading and teaching the importance of reading impart a value. We are teaching the skill, but are we teaching the value?

Today, our distinguished panelists and guests will help us bring three questions into focus. First, what is the extent of this phenomenon of aliteracy: is it a significant and growing problem? Second, is literacy an important value? And third, if indeed it is an important value, how can we ensure its survival?

MR. THIMMESCH: Today we will explore a new form of the literacy problem— aliterates, people who can read but won't. Because literacy is a complicated question, we will focus only on that growing segment of the population that is gradually turning away from reading. Television seems to be the ready explanation for this phenomenon. Daniel Boorstin, the Librarian of Congress, has called television the next great crisis in human consciousness. We know that by age fifteen, the average American child has spent more time in front of a television set than in the classroom or in doing homework. Now a generation of youngsters is coming along that also spends many additional hours playing games in video parlors or playing video games at home. Television news claims as many viewers as this nation's 1,710 newspapers have readers. While television news is expanding, newspaper circulation remains static—it fails to keep pace with the population. In 1970, daily circulation of U.S. newspapers was 62.1 million; in 1981, it was 61.4 million, a drop of 700,000. If we take into account population growth, newspaper circulation

1

actually declined about 7 percent in this twelve-year period. Because the newspaper is the most commonly used print medium, we must ask what this decline in newspaper reading means to developing public policy. Television news views itself as essentially a headline service, richly complemented with vivid visuals. Television creates images, characters, even stereotypes. More cops, judges, and private eyes inhabit the world of television than enter our real-life experience, where people sell insurance and pave streets and grow crops. Far more violence occurs on television than in real life. Small wonder that studies show heavy television viewers to be more suspicious of people than those described as heavy readers. People who rely on television to size up political candidates make far more subjective judgments than people who rely largely on written accounts about those candidates and the issues. It is even possible to conjure up an Orwellian world where lower income and minority people become television's biggest audience while the people who do a lot of reading become the decision makers, even a sort of elite.

Of course, it is too simplistic to cast television as the villain and the printed word as the hero. The situation is, however, serious enough that newspaper publishers are engaged in a major effort to encourage reading. Our panelists are concerned not only with improving newspaper readership in quantity and quality, but also with broadening the base of all forms of reading.

The Nonreading Culture

Robert M. Wilson

I became aware of aliteracy in my work with the American Newspapers Publishers Association. While working there with writers and educators, I saw the drastic decline in readership of newspapers. At the time we considered this trend a problem of literacy, but, as has already been demonstrated to you, literacy is not the problem.

Degrees of Literacy

Literacy as defined by the Census Bureau is an odd thing. It changes every ten years by definition, and comparative data are difficult to find. Basically, though, people who can read at about the fourth-grade level are deemed literate. Because a person might be able to read at a fourth-grade level and not be able to function very well in our society, a new term evolved, "functional literacy." This expression means that a person who can read school books might not be able to read the materials needed for success outside the schoolroom. In Maryland, for example, we have a functional literacy test, which is a requirement for graduation from high school, and almost everybody passes that test. Perhaps, then, functional literacy is not the problem either. We then came to believe that many who can read do not: the aliterates. Perhaps we will some day see two cultures develop in our society—one a reading culture and one a nonreading culture.

Why People Avoid Reading

Why, then, do those who can read choose not to? We do not have very good data, but we do have some good guesses. One reason might be related to the content of the newspaper. On a recent Sunday morning, I opened my newspaper and was confronted with photographs of the bodies in the streets in Beirut and scenes from the funeral of Princess Grace and then read grim news about the economy. Now I'm a reader who reads, but I laid the paper aside so that I could enjoy my breakfast in comfort. Although I'm not complaining about the selection of articles in the newspaper, some are. In a recent seminar

3

here for Kinney Shoe Company, as reported in the *Washington Post*, the consultant who travels all over the nation helping the employees become better salespeople says that if they want to stay positive, they should stop reading the newspaper. He contends that they cannot read and absorb the news in detail and then have a positive attitude at work.

Another possible explanation for aliteracy is that schools focus on sub-skills instead of on the global reading act, an approach that might rob our children of some of the enjoyment in reading. At the University of Maryland reading clinic we require teachers in training for reading positions to demonstrate their skills by working with students in our clinic. The children that come to this clinic are school-aged children with serious reading handicaps. Most of them, I believe, have the skills, but because they do not use them, they appear to be nonreaders. As we focus on the skills that the students can demonstrate successfully, we get impressive results. We can sometimes reverse their attitude entirely. This past summer, for instance, one child said, "I finally figured out what you're doing—you're sneaking the reading in on us." They were using directions for making pizza, and after they made it, they read the directions again, so he said we were sneaking reading in on them.

The third possible explanation is the declining support for the public schools. This tragic weakening of support for education occurs at the national level, the state level, and the local level, where schools receive less and less support from the communities they serve. An interesting poll published in *Phi Delta Kappa* magazine ranked the major social priorities, and the highest priority of the people participating in that poll was support for education—not crime prevention, not concerns over the economy. The fact that some people who can read but don't is troublesome because not only do these people avoid the reading act and have no access to the materials available, but also their skills actually diminish. In the end, these people may even lose the ability to read with understanding. I liken it to swimming. As a youngster I swam a lot, I took Red Cross courses, I was a lifeguard, and I considered myself a very good swimmer. As I got busier and busier, I spent less and less time swimming. Today, I go to the pool and I have a hard time swimming one lap. If you don't use the skill, it diminishes.

Aliteracy and the Newspaper Industry

Shirley Foutz

The problem of aliteracy is of great concern to the newspaper industry. As noted in the preceding paper, newspaper circulation has grown only half as fast as the number of households in the past three decades. Many factors contributed to this decline in newspaper reading, but rather than delineate them, I will discuss some of the ways that we are coping with this readership situation in Richmond, Virginia. First, we are changing to offset printing to improve the quality of reproduction. We are reducing the size for more convenient handling of the newspaper. We are using more color and larger, clearer photographs. We also plan to use a format with six columns instead of an eight or nine. All of these changes will make our newspapers less threatening and more appealing to readers.

Newspapers in Education

My primary objective today, however, is to describe a national effort to alleviate the readership problem. Nearly one-half or about 800 of the daily newspapers in the United States are involved in this program, which we have called "Newspapers in Education," or NIE. Although newspapers have been used sporadically in schools for many, many years, and the *New York Times* has had a long-standing school program, newspapers and educators have joined forces only since 1956 to increase the planned use of newspapers in schools as part of NIE. NIE, sponsored nationally by the American Newspapers Publishers Association Foundation, works to achieve three goals: first, to encourage in young people a continuing desire and ability to read a newspaper critically and reflectively; second, to encourage in young people a concern for public issues and the motivation to involve themselves in our self-governing process; and third, to encourage in young people an understanding of the role of a free press in our society.

How are these goals being implemented in NIE programs? I can speak with authority concerning only one, the program sponsored by the *Richmond Times Dispatch* and the *Richmond News Leader*. From its very beginning,

5

top management has viewed our program not as a present circulation builder, but as an investment in future readership.

Let me briefly describe our program, which is fairly representative of NIE programs nationally. As a formal program, it began in 1974 when I was hired as its first coordinator. Since that time, we have grown into an educational services department of three, managing all the school programs sponsored by our papers. For the first six years, though, I labored alone, traveling to all forty-seven school divisions of central Virginia composing our circulation area. Now that we are better staffed and better organized, we reach all of our 14,500 teachers at least every other month with our newsletter *Teacher's Features*. One person, usually an administrator, from each of the forty-seven divisions serves as a liaison, relaying to teachers news of our free teacher-training workshops, our ten-cent newspapers delivered to the schools, our free instructional materials, slide presentations, tours, parent workshops, and other services. In every succeeding year of our program's operation, the number of newspapers being used in the schools and the number of requests for teacher training have increased. We sponsor both in-service and graduate credit courses called "Effective Teaching with the Newspaper," which I teach in conjunction with faculty at Virginia Commonwealth University, Longwood College, and the University of Richmond. The focus of the teacher training, whatever the location, is not on teaching about the newspaper per se, but on implementing it as an instructional tool to help teachers meet their classroom objectives. Of course, we do not advocate throwing out the textbooks, but rather integrating an up-to-date, highly relevant tool to bridge the gap between the classroom and the world outside.

The Newspaper in the Classroom

Teachers at all levels are using our newspapers. Primary teachers find interesting uses for the many pictures and numbers, creating cut-and-paste activities for the children. Reading teachers use the newspaper for teaching all the skills, but particularly for teaching the comprehension skills of critical reading— those skills absolutely necessary for students to become discerning readers not only of newspapers, but also of all other printed materials. Social studies teachers use the newspaper to update textbooks in economics and law-related studies. Math teachers use it for application of math skills, especially those built around such practical problems as shopping for groceries, buying a car, applying for a job, or figuring interest on loans. Remedial reading teachers have noticed that students do not feel as threatened by newspapers as they seem to be by textbooks. Remedial readers themselves are not embarrassed to be seen using them because they carry an adult image. Students also like them because they deal in reality, in the here and now, even if much of the news is bad. Motivation for reading and for discussion is built in. With many

6

sections and features, newspapers contain something of interest for almost every student.

The results of three national research projects conducted in 1977, 1980, and 1982 under the auspices of the Newspaper Readership Project are revealing. They indicate that students who use newspapers in schools are more interested in public issues, have more knowledge of social and political issues, and, perhaps the most important for our purposes here, are more likely to read newspapers as adults.

In closing, I will share something that Walter Cronkite said in 1979 when he was speaking to the National School Boards Association. He called on newspapers, television, radio, and schools to work together. He said,

> You, the schools, and I, the media, are in the same game and we have problems. We are both in the business of providing the information that will enable the people to intelligently play a role in their society. That translates in a democracy to their ability to intelligently exercise their franchise as citizens. Your job is to train them to think, ours is to supply the raw material to feed the thinking process.

Those of us directly involved in newspaper and education programs believe we are working with both the school and the print media in a way that will develop newspaper-reading habits and intelligent citizens who will exercise their franchise.

Television and the Aliteracy Problem

Lynne Grasz

For over thirty years, many people have believed that television would mean the end of reading, just as it was predicted earlier that television would be the end of radio and that television would be the end of movies. Today radio, especially FM, is at its highest and strongest point in history. Movies are enjoying their biggest box-office summer in the history of the industry, especially with *E.T.*; and last year more than 41,000 book titles were published compared with some 8,600 in 1950. That number represents almost a fivefold increase in thirty years, demonstrating once again that new technology does not automatically displace the old. Instead of television's advent signaling the end of books, the two media now enjoy a natural complementary relationship.

Read More about It

In 1979, Dr. Daniel J. Boorstin, the Librarian of Congress, met with Gene Mater, senior vice president of policy at the CBS Broadcast Group. Dr. Boorstin, earlier quoted as calling television "the next great crisis in human consciousness," suggested linking the printed word and television. CBS accepted that challenge back in 1979 to use the popularity and appeal of television to stimulate further reading. The title selected for this project demonstrated what CBS and the Library of Congress wanted to achieve: We wanted the public to read more about it. Thus, the "Read More about It" book project resulted from that joint effort begun over four years ago. The project reflects the interest of CBS in encouraging and developing an informed public. Television is being used to its fullest potential by tapping its many opportunities to reach wide audiences of young and old, to inform, to stimulate, to motivate, and to remind people that viewing can be supplemented with one of the oldest sources of information and entertainment, reading. The project began in November 1979 with an adaptation of *All Quiet on the Western Front* on the CBS Television Network and has been rerun once. At the conclusion of the broadcast, one of the actors in the show, Richard Thomas, appeared in a special announcement to tell viewers of several books on the history of World

War I and its impact. The particular selections were suggested by the Library of Congress. He also referred viewers to their local libraries and bookstores for other books; in addition, a complete list of sixteen books was made available to libraries, bookstores, and all CBS Television Network affiliates. This project has continued for four years.

Because our purpose is to entertain as well as to educate, we do not always choose literary classics. I will give an example of a "spot" used to publicize a show called, "The Royal Romance of Charles and Diana." This thirty-second announcement, which will run this evening, will be viewed on the CBS Television Network by millions of people and should arouse considerable interest:

> If you'd like to read more about the royal romance, the Library of Congress suggests these books: *Princess* by Robert Lasson, *Debrett's Book of the Royal Wedding* by Hubert Vicars, *Two Centuries of Royal Weddings* by Christopher Warring. These and many other good books are available at your local library and bookstore; visit them. They'll be happy to help you read more about it.

Stewart Granger, who plays the role of Prince Philip this evening, delivered those lines. We always try to choose one of the major stars to present the television spots.

Diversity of Productions. Since 1979, we have produced thirty of these broadcasts covering a wide range of subject matter, of interest to audiences both young and old. To illustrate the diversity of the programs, I will name some of our presentations. During the first year, we gave "All Quiet on the Western Front." In addition, our initial season included the "Mayflower, the Pilgrim's Progress"; "The Gift"; "The Boy Who Drank Too Much"; "The Ordeal of Dr. Mudd"; "Gauguin the Savage"; "The Henderson Monster," dealing with genetics; "Gideon's Trumpet," with Henry Fonda; "The American Film Institute's Salute to Jimmy Stewart"; and a show on the funny papers, "The Fantastic Funnies," which was rerun recently. During the 1980–1981 season, we did the Country Music Awards, "Little Lord Fauntleroy," "A Tale of Two Cities," "The Bunker," "The American Film Institute's Salute to Fred Astaire," and "The Pride of Jessie Hallam," with Johnny Cash, which is about an illiterate man who teaches himself to read. Last year, we did fourteen specials, which included a magic show with David Copperfield, "Skokie" with Danny Kaye, and "The Marva Collins Story," with Cicely Tyson. Many of these shows were nominated for Emmys. Others in the season were Walt Disney's "One Man's Dream," and "Bill," with Mickey Rooney (both the show and Mickey Rooney won an Emmy), Agatha Christie's "Murder Is Easy" with Helen Hayes, "The Kennedy Center Honors," which is a big event here in Washington, "Baryshnikov in Hollywood," "The Tony

Awards," "Ivanhoe," "The Wall," "Oliver Twist," and our first animated special, "Charlie Brown's Celebration"—with the spot performed by Snoopy and Charlie Brown for this last one.

We have just announced our 1982–1983 season, making this our most ambitious year ever. To date, we have produced thirty specials, and we're going to do thirty just this coming year, bringing to sixty the total since the beginning of "Read More about It." Hundreds of book titles will, therefore, have exposure to national audiences, giving the public a heightened awareness of books and reading. The lists of books mentioned on the air are not compiled by CBS; they are selected by bibliographers and reference librarians on the staff of the Library of Congress. These specialists also choose the books for a larger list of in-print book titles, giving a variety of perspectives on every subject.

Scripts in the Classroom. CBS is involved in another project besides "Read More about It": the "CBS Television Reading Program," the script project that we do with local CBS stations and with newspapers. CBS became interested in the television script reading concept in 1976. Simply stated, the concept is to follow the dialogue of a popular television program with a transcript. Teachers and students originally used the scripts to read while watching programs on a playback unit in the classroom. The use of these transcripts as regular reading matter resulted in considerable improvement in student reading scores, and, in some cases, the reading levels jumped as much as three grades. The expansion of the script reading program, however, was limited by the availability of classroom hardware. The next logical step in this program, then, was to take it to where the hardware was, the children's homes. In 1976, CBS began exploring the television script reading concept on a pilot basis in three cities. I happened to be involved in the pilot study in St. Louis at the CBS station there, KMOX-TV, where our first program was "A Circle of Children." This presentation, with Jane Alexander, was a story of autistic children. The reading program became so popular among the teachers, students, and advertisers who paid for the scripts that it was expanded the following year, in 1977, to include twenty-two affiliated stations. Now a nationwide project, it numbers over 30 million students as participants. It was designed to help elementary and secondary school students improve their reading skills and to motivate them to further reading by building upon their enthusiasm for television.

This last year, for example, we did "M*A*S*H*" because we know the show is popular with children. For this program we produced a bilingual script, printed in Spanish as well as in English. To supplement the scripts, we produced a teacher's guide describing reading projects for the class to participate in; depending on the show, a script may be used by a drama class for acting out the parts or it may form the basis for classroom discussion. As a rule, the students read the script in advance in class, they take it home, and often, we found, the entire family sits down to follow the dialogue through the program. Sometimes, the parents feel as if they are helping their children with homework.

I have described just two of the reading projects that CBS is involved in; we have many more. We at CBS believe that a broadcasting organization can link the pleasure, power, and excitement of reading to television and can provide the opportunities and sufficient inducements for the aliterates to want to read.

The "Reading to Learn" Approach

John Campbell

Several key terms have recurred in the preceding papers. Dr. Wilson referred to the global aspect of reading, an important notion if we consider reading a cognitive process as well as a psychological process. Cognitively, we break the complex reading act into 200 or 300 or 400 skills, depending on the approach, and then we teach each separate skill exhaustively. Through some mysterious process, students are supposed to integrate and coordinate all of those processes. The act of learning to read, therefore, embodies many goals and objectives that educators have set for students. What we need to emphasize in the schools and in teacher training is the "reading to learn" approach because reading is, after all, a way of gathering information, of making decisions, and even of thinking.

Reading as a Psychological Activity

If reading is considered a psychological act, then we need to be concerned about developing positive interests and habits, something that does not occur simply by mandate. We cannot decree that by June 1 an individual will have developed good reading habits, measurable by how many books he checks out. If we look at the decision-making process introduced in an earlier paper, we see that many different factors influence the individual's decision to read. The home, for example, can be a positive influence as demonstrated in the instance already cited in which linking television programs with reading activities became a family project. "Roots" inspired entire school systems to tie television presentations to serious work within the school.

Of course, we also need school systems dedicated to helping children develop positive reading habits and willing to provide time for the children to read. Research has shown that children are given very little time to read in schools. Those with reading problems are very rarely given opportunities to read meaningful units. They are given sentences, or they are told to break down words. When I teach the five-year-olds on my soccer team how to shoot, how to dribble, or how to kick, they become impatient; they want to play a game, not to look at each individual technical segment of how to play soccer. The same is true of the reading act.

Instructional Practices. We need to examine the instructional practices in the schools, and there are many different ways of doing that. Project "To Read," for example, worked with nonreading juvenile offenders by giving them books. "Hooked on Books," an English program and a newspaper program started by a Dr. Fader from Michigan, is another program that works. Children are exposed to using books for specific, interesting purposes. They are not told to find the unfamiliar words on page eight and look them up, or to find all the words on page fourteen with the short "a" sound and write them in a list. They must be asked to think about what they read, not just to go through the motions of naming the main character, the setting, and the key events. Who are the main characters in "Laverne and Shirley," where do they come from, what brewery do they work for? They will tell you. Does Joanie really love Chachi? The children know and can tell you why. Of course these children use thinking skills. It is not the thinking skills that are in question. Much of the problem is a psychological one in which the children never experience the act of reading and find it rewarding.

Community Outreach. Library readership is up, partly because the libraries have a tremendous community outreach program that often involves the co-operation of the schools. I recently happened to pick up at the library books *about* the old *for* the young. What powerful bibliotherapy can come out of this kind of material! Countless subjects lend themselves to this special sort of insight. The schools need to be more aware of compelling topics and to capitalize on them. The school system needs to cooperate more, and those in charge of teacher training need to communicate the possibilities to prospective teachers and to nurture and reinforce ways that we can teach children to read and develop positive habits.

Television cannot be blamed for children's lack of interest in reading. The children who spend approximately fifty-three hours a week watching television do not do so in a vacuum. Normally, they watch within the context of a family environment for some of those hours. Educators, then, need to work more with parents in helping children to think analytically about what they are watching. Plots, characters, and time-settings appear in both books and television and make good starting points for thought and discussion.

Just as we need to work with the school systems, so do we also need to work with television and other media. We need to foster opportunities for students to gain enjoyment without being tested to death on the specifics, allowing them to talk about such subjective responses as whether they liked the book or not. The only way we can develop strong habits is if we feel comfortable and successful at a habit. I do not attempt to fix electrical gadgets because I have never been successful at it, but I do read because I feel comfortable about that.

Teachers and Parents as Reading Models

We need, too, to work with teachers as readers. Dr. Robert Duffey from the University of Maryland has reported that teachers for the most part are not habitual readers. It is difficult to impart the love of reading or even a positive attitude about reading unless one has it himself. Parents above all need to be models. Passively viewing television or movies will not set the needed example. Parents can become involved in many ways to help their children become good readers. Children come to school with a love for reading, wanting to hear stories, wanting to read books. When my five-year-old picks out books, he chooses ones with big, thick covers. To him, they are a status symbol, but he loves to look at the pages. We also know that as the years go on in school, the interest in books declines, a tendency carried into the adult years. Many adults lack that positive attitude toward reading, reading only when they have to. As adults, they are reading for work as they read for school when they were young.

If, therefore, we seek to develop only the cognitive elements of the reading act at the expense of psychological satisfactions, we are losing the very key to developing life-long readers.

Discussion

DR. LEVINE: One of the basic questions that we are addressing is how our citizenry gets its information. For an informed process of decision making, this is a very basic question. Do we, in fact, have a less informed citizenry because individuals are reading less? Are they getting their information from several sources, and does it matter from which source the information comes? Does, for example, watching television provide a frame of reference different from reading newspapers in terms of information? Does it develop a different set of skills or reinforce the use of different cognitive processes in the individual? If so, are the differences important?

Ms. FOUTZ: In the same message that Walter Cronkite gave to that National School Boards Association in 1979 that I referred to earlier, he discussed the fact that television news coverage is really more a matter of headlines and leads, the first paragraph of a news story, and said that if we are to get the whole story, especially what language arts teachers would call the supporting details, then we need to go to the newspaper for background. Television's approach to news is different from a newspaper's approach, but it can well be complementary. The written word makes it easier for a person to think about what has been presented and to come to his own conclusions about a situation because he can return to that article and see those details and evaluate the information. In other words, critical thinking comes more naturally in reading.

DR. WILSON: In addition, newspaper reading is an individual act in which the reader constantly challenges the print. If a reader thinks about the way he selects articles to read in a newspaper, he finds that he is always challenging the print, predicting the content, and entering into an active process, a healthy reading process. When I pick up the morning newspaper, the first thing I do is look through the headlines to decide which articles I want to read. I reject some, select others, and predict which articles will carry information important to me. I will read only as much of an article as I need to answer my questions, and then I can quit. I can pace myself to read very fast, or I can pace myself to read a paragraph, stop and think about it, talk to my wife about it, and go back and read it again. It is available to read again, a very important advantage. I can save it, I can take it home, I can put it in my den, I can read it next week. I have a big newspaper scrapbook where I save important newspaper articles. I started saving articles during World War II, and I have accumulated some really interesting reading. I get that book out and look it over again and again. Being able to look back and having the option to stop, think, and challenge are very important.

DR. CAMPBELL: Dr. Wilson's answer comes from a person who reads and predicts. I want to know how to get students in high schools and junior high schools to start reading actively rather than just going through the act with the minimum mental effort. Many students can relate what was literally on the page, but they need more practice in evaluating what they read. The critical thinking is what is lacking.

As a result of the recent political campaigns, we just generated enough reading material to furnish the basis for teaching critical reading skills for ten years. Nobody is for fewer jobs or poorer housing—everybody is for the same thing—but how do you go about evaluating politicians' claims? If one starts to practice critical reading early, then I think that practice will continue. Although my father never finished eighth grade, we had five daily newspapers coming to our house, allowing me the luxury of early exposure to newspapers. All of us need this early and consistent exposure so that we can build up a storehouse of knowledge and habits.

QUESTION: Ms. Grasz, has any research examined the relationship between the CBS spots and the sales of the books mentioned by the speakers?

MS. GRASZ: We have not done any systematic research on that. Through feedback from the librarians and students, we have found that the books mentioned are checked out more frequently. We have also found that there is a heavy checkout of other books related to the same subject.

To refer to an earlier question concerning where the public gets its information, I should mention research from the Television Information Office indicating that more people get their news from television than from any other information source. These studies also show that newspaper readership is declining. The afternoon newspapers are particularly hard hit because so many people watch the television news when they get home, rather than read an afternoon paper.

Television news cannot be anything more than a headline service because after the commercials are removed from a half-hour show, only about twenty-two minutes are left for news. To quote Walter Cronkite again, in a speech he remarked that if he substituted the *New York Times* for one of his scripts, he could not read more than a column in the allotted time because reading speed on television is limited by the audience's slower comprehension rate. There is, though, strong demand in this country for more news, which is the motivation for the three networks' going to overnight news services. This demand also explains the emergence of the cable news network. People are hungry for news, and the logical extension of this need is to supplement television news with reading, either a news magazine or a newspaper.

QUESTION: Should secondary or higher education adopt the approach of St. John's College at Annapolis, which for its four-year, liberal arts degree still teaches by using the classics? Incidentally, some of the other great universities like Harvard and Yale are perhaps beginning to go in that direction.

DR. CAMPBELL: Whether or not we go in the direction of the classics, for the majority of students in secondary schools, we do need to bring more books into the classroom. I do not advocate the St. John's Great Books approach per se, but we do need to have more books in the schools and time for reading the books.

QUESTION: Dr. Campbell mentioned briefly the importance of community outreach and of helping the parents to become involved in reading. I am especially concerned about the low-income parent and the parent who has not completed a secondary education. How can we help, or what strategies can any member of the panel suggest whereby we could help the parents to learn to help their children become readers?

MS. FOUTZ: We have done some of this work in Richmond, not as much as I would like because of time constraints, but we are conducting workshops with parents. Ostensibly, the purpose is to show parents ways they can use the newspaper to help their children learn, but what happens at the same time is that the parents themselves are learning how to use the newspaper. We usually incorporate consumer types of activities that would be of real benefit to the kinds of adults you mentioned.

QUESTION: The panel seems inclined to define almost any form of reading as different from the state of aliteracy. Today's bestseller list, the nonfiction list at least, is full of books about dead cats and diets. These are books, and people are buying them. Does this level of reading constitute aliteracy?

Also, if people buy newspapers, do they read them? We do not really know if they read anything more than the headlines if they do buy them, but by some definitions if they get newspapers, just any newspaper, then they are not in the aliterate class. A new newspaper came out just this week that looks like television in print to me, and maybe that is the best way to sell newspapers. On the other hand, where does literacy end and aliteracy begin?

17

DR. WILSON: Aliteracy is really rather difficult to define. What we have are multitudes of people who read nothing. They do not buy newspapers, they do not read newspapers, they do not buy books, they do not read books. They are reading nothing, and I would submit that it is better to read something written at a sixth-grade level and read it regularly than not to read anything at all. Most of the articles in the *Reader's Digest* are written at a sixth-grade or seventh-grade level, and people that read those articles are at least practicing their reading skills. Maybe the material is not especially challenging. Newspapers are written around the seventh or eighth-grade levels, depending upon the section of the newspaper, and I enjoy reading the newspaper. I practice good reading habits, and am not overly concerned about how difficult the material is.

QUESTION: Why would people do better to read this sort of material than they would to watch the equivalent on television?

DR. LEVINE: Even more basic questions come to mind: what is the value of reading? What are we losing if we are not reading? What happens if we do not have a reading population? Is there a difference between reading the "printed television" sort of newspaper and reading some other newspaper or between reading books about dead cats or reading classic literature? What is lost when we stop reading the classics—personally, individually, and as a society? I cannot answer these questions, but they are important for us to think about. We seem to assume that we are losing something, but we are unable to articulate exactly what it is.

COMMENT: We are losing the critical thinking skills, the predicting skills, and the argumentation skills that come into play when we read a newspaper. Newspaper reading is a personal process and a challenging process. The reader must actively participate in the act, and that activity stimulates thinking.

QUESTION: What evidence, other than stagnant newspaper circulation, is there that reading is declining? In a previous paper, it was noted that the number of book titles quadrupled and that magazine circulation apparently has climbed way up. Is there evidence from libraries, for instance, that reading is going down?

COMMENT: It is difficult to find statistical evidence to prove that reading is declining. Library usership is up. Does that mean that more people are using a library, or does it mean that a certain segment of the population keeps going back to the library? One approach that I have taken with junior high and secondary schools is to stand outside of the school to see how many books are going home; I have seen very few in many schools.

QUESTION: Might not a simple explanation be that teachers are assigning the students less to read, that there is less homework? You do not have to move the problem to a cosmic realm along with values and questions of aliteracy. Teachers are just expecting less reading and homework from their students. Then this becomes a manageable problem of the school curriculum and teachers. If this is the root of the problem, wouldn't the simplest way to solve it be to stiffen the school curriculum and expect children to read more?

COMMENT: In response to your last comment, we are encouraging teachers in our teacher education training to have children read for periods of time everyday; we call it "sustained reading." This trend is prevalent in the United States today, and I think it is really a healthy one. Usually, in a given period of time everyday, in every classroom of the school, all activity stops and everybody reads—in high schools as well as in elementary and junior high schools.

They bring books that they want to read, and they are not questioned on the reading; they are reading purely for enjoyment, trying to develop that habit of reading. In a study in Lewisdale Elementary School in Prince George's County, Maryland, we measured time on task during sustained reading as opposed to time on task during teacher-directed activities. We found time on task during sustained reading to be almost 100 percent. Children were reading books that they wanted to read with no particular requirement to prove how much comprehension they managed. The trend allowing children to read books of their choice without the threat of testing for comprehension is really a healthy one. Our clinic takes children who claim they cannot read anything, and we give them sustained reading for twenty minutes out of a period of two and a half hours.

MS. FOUTZ: Many schools in our area are using newspapers during what we call SSR time or "sustained silent reading time," and we are seeing the same kinds of interest in reading there for both books or newspapers. When the teacher uses newspapers, though, she or he almost has to allow time in class for some reading because the students are frankly so interested in the content that if the teacher does not provide them this time at the beginning of the class period, they will not pay attention to the lesson planned for that day.

QUESTION: Does the motivation of CBS in mounting its "Read More about It" campaign, which may serve a fine public purpose, stem from enlightened self-interest in view of its position in the book publishing field?

MS. GRASZ: No, CBS is divided into several groups: the broadcast group is one profit center, and CBS Publishing is another. We thought through this question very carefully because we did not want to appear to use this program as a vehicle to sell our own books. We are sensitive to this issue, and for this reason the books are selected by the Library of Congress. I have nothing to do with the book selection.

QUESTION: Most people here would probably agree with the points that have been made: improving reading is important whether it occurs through the school curriculum, through cooperation between television stations and teachers in terms of developing programs, or through strengthening the basic skills so that comprehension and critical thinking are enhanced. No one disputes these points. Where is the evidence, though, to indicate that reading has declined in this country in the population that reads material besides newspapers? A number of trends would seem to indicate precisely the opposite case. With more children graduating from high schools than ever before, with more people going on to higher education than ever before, with more people involved in adult education than ever before, inevitably more, rather than less, reading is involved.

If the issue here is reading in relation to decision making, then perhaps a slightly different kind of focus is needed. A reverse in newspaper reading is unlikely, but even if one were possible, it might not solve the problem. With the exception of a few large newspapers in some of our major cities, local newspapers do not really provide the quality that will give people the kinds of information on which to base good decisions anyway. In decision making, therefore, shouldn't the real emphasis be on improving the quality of television news coverage? This approach might have greater impact, not that I dismiss in any way the importance of reading and improving reading.

DR. LEVINE: I commented earlier on that phenomenon that you're identifying: that more and more high school students are graduating, and the reading skills are being taught. I question, however, whether those skills are in fact being effectively applied. The question that remains in my mind is how the developments in personal reading habits will affect the decision-making process. It isn't clear to me whether the information that one gets from television news is comparable to the information one gets from newspapers and whether television can really be made richer in its content than what is available in the average daily newspaper.

DR. WILSON: Several have asked if there really is a problem. In the beginning, we established that we were doing a better job with literacy and that we were doing a better job teaching functional reading. We are, though, turning many readers off. That is a big problem.

Although I do not have all the evidence here at hand, I will cite some supporting facts. I became interested in aliteracy through my work with ANPA, where I realized the magnitude of the problem nationally as reflected in declining newspaper readership. Then, Dr. Duffey at the University of Maryland did a study mentioned previously indicating that teachers are not reading. That is a serious situation and a problem that must be dealt with. Finally, a recent study of college graduates found that the average college graduate had not read a book in the four years after graduating.

QUESTION: Ms. Grasz, can you comment on the network news organizations in providing more in-depth news? I notice, for instance, that the documentary is becoming almost a rarity on television.

MS. GRASZ: The history of television news is not a long one. The first television news broadcast was made by Douglas Edwards—a fifteen-minute program in the mid-1950s. Fifteen minutes was the standard broadcast forum until the mid-1960s when we went to half an hour. CBS was the first to use the half-hour news format, with Walter Cronkite. Then local news began to follow suit.

Local news became very important because traditionally the top station in the news ratings is number one on all daytime broadcasting, and the top-rated show can sell its advertising time for the highest price. The first station to adopt an expanded newscast was a CBS station, KNXT, in Los Angeles, with a two-and-a-half-hour news block in the afternoon. There was a demand for more news in the area, and this station developed the most successful format. At this point, all the stations started going "live at 5," and the news time kept growing longer.

Now with the overnight news mentioned earlier and early morning news programs like "Early Today," the "Today Show," "Good Morning, America," and the CBS "Morning Program," there is more and more coverage. The problem from a news standpoint is that there is a lot of news happening.

In an article that I read recently, the author observed that these early morning shows are becoming more feature oriented. They are not really hard news shows. This trend is reflected in some of the popular magazines like *People Magazine* and the *National Enquirer*. People are interested in celebrities, a reason for *USA Today*'s popularity.

With its overnight news, CBS is serving a diversity of people who want news during the evening hours or swing shifts, college students who are up late, for instance. We want to reach those who are normally home but not using television. It is a question of a profit bottom line: are advertisers willing to pay for those demographics in the middle of the night?

As for documentaries, I am not certain that there are fewer. CBS does quite a few documentaries during the year. If "CBS Reports," "Universe," and even "Sixty Minutes"—a series of three or four mini-documentaries strung together in entertainment format—are counted, there are a fair number. News is the hot television item today.

21

QUESTION: As a sociologist and teacher of sociology at the university level, I can assure those who wonder if any evidence indicates that reading is declining that indeed it is. My classroom was composed almost entirely of people incapable of reading the college-level text. The book publishers of college textbooks are producing succeeding generations of textbooks that simplify on the previous simplification until the result is almost a comic book approach to complex sociological concepts.

Perhaps, though, we ought to look with a flinty eye at why such a conference as this was called at all. We have heard from book publishers, newspaper people, teachers, and other "print junkies," who have a vested interest in increasing reading and in saving this technique, the technology of literacy. Other people have raised the issue that I would hope to consider a little more closely: that is, exactly what advantage do reading and literacy hold in terms of helping us to process information? What does reading give us that is of some social advantage that cannot be obtained through other media? Is it entirely certain that we cannot have a functioning society with an oral-aural method of communication, where we use television and its still unexploited resources for communication? Television, radio, and other electronic ways of processing information rapidly retrieve information and present it to people. Is it impossible to conceive of a generation that has received its knowledge of the world and itself through television?

Does reading really make a practical difference for some other value we cherish, democratic institutions for instance? Is it that people truly cannot recognize and deal with the complexities of the issues if they are not literate in the old-fashioned sense? Is it that nonreaders cannot construe incoming information? Can we no longer come to a public consensus through dialogue if people don't read? What evidence at all supports the proposition that reading is not just sufficient but necessary for conducting the polity?

DR. CAMPBELL: We do not need to separate reading from television or from the oral aspects of communication. What I see is a decline in the value that school-aged children have placed on reading; reading, as another way to get information, should be emphasized as such. Information from television should be supplemented with the more in-depth information available in print. I learn about myself by reading certain types of books, and I make decisions based upon what I read.

COMMENT: Of course you do, but couldn't you do all of that without the reading? Following the lead of C.S. Peirce and William James, what is the practical consequence of reading that is different from and more effective, more efficient, and more valuable somehow than the practical consequence of constituting your mind yourself, so that you could receive your information through other channels?

Ms. FOUTZ: We know that we learn differently. Some of us may well be able to learn all we need through auditory means; but many of us, especially those of us in my generation who were taught to learn through reading, will probably not be able to learn everything we need to know unless we can see it on the printed page.

QUESTION: But what is the underlying difference between these two ways of learning?

COMMENT: I might suggest a difference: a person cannot talk back to a television program unless it is a QB system. What you are bringing up here is the whole art of dialogue.

QUESTION: As someone whose business it is to teach adults to read, I am concerned that some of the previous comments presuppose we have been a literate society all along; I do not believe that that is so. Some of the decline we see in reading among the general population correlates with our efforts toward universal education. Perhaps as we make a greater effort to educate everybody, a smaller percentage of those who are educated are going to be readers. In the past people who were going to be readers anyway were generally the ones who remained in school.

Our view of how people spent their time before television may not be accurate. I recently reread *Ethan Frome*, by Edith Wharton, and I was struck by how they spent their evenings: they watched each other sew in the kitchen. They didn't talk, they didn't read—they just sat and watched each other sew. Can we really be getting less information about the world by watching television in the evenings?

DR. WILSON: The notions of a decline in reading and of a new reading problem did not originate with me. I have never contended that this problem is a new one. We simply did not pay attention to it before when we were concentrating on setting up literacy and functional reading standards. We did not address the issue of what people were or were not reading. I do not see aliteracy as a new problem; we are looking at it for the first time, perhaps.

QUESTION: It is difficult for me to conceive of handling the most common things without reading. Classified ads or any kind of large-scale advertising would be difficult to achieve from the mouth and the picture to the ear. History would be difficult to handle if all one could do was plug into a half-hour show that was done twenty-five or thirty years ago. When I look up a word in the dictionary, I want to do that with my eyes. I want to have my own choices as Dr. Wilson noted, choice and challenge, the process of working with print.

The television age may have a larger common pool of information, but with more information at their disposal, fewer people are voting. Studies do show that newspaper readers are more frequent voters. What the larger problem is and whether the decline in reading has any bearing on the percentage of voters are important matters.

MR. THIMMESCH: It is interesting that the voting in the presidental elections since 1960 has dropped about 3 percent each election. It would be interesting to relate reading to the determination of public policy and the voting act.

COMMENT: Several studies have documented this correlation. The one I saw cited most recently was in California. I am not asserting a particular point, just a concern about the relation of sources of information to people's reluctance to act on it.

DR. LEVINE: Although I don't have data from studies on this subject, I see reading as an active, mentally engaging process while television watching is a much less active process. To speculate for a moment, I wonder if taking an active role in the political process correlates with the active role in which people acquire their information. Perhaps something goes on in the reading process—the choice, the selectivity, the individualness of it—that is characteristic of the person and is carried out in his political role. The question is interesting, and I would like to see reports on the subject.

COMMENT: One of the facts that we are overlooking is that we can process information from reading at the speed of thought while we process information from television at the speed of speech and sometimes very slowly.

QUESTION: Do we have any percentage, or can we even guess a percentage of aliteracy? Will aliteracy potentially make a class division in this country? Does aliteracy in any way indicate that our general level of culture is in decline, or is there any way to measure that?

DR. WILSON: We cannot determine whether our culture is declining or whether aliteracy is a bigger problem than it was before. It is simply a problem we have identified now that we had not identified before.

DR. CAMPBELL: As we gain more information about this particular problem, the potential may appear for some type of class distinction. As the title of this panel suggests, the decision-making process may be endangered. The problem itself is not new, but we have identified it only recently.

The people who become involved in the democratic process of voting have made decisions and seem to have the background of experience and information to make those decisions. Maybe the more a person reads, the more information he has to make critical decisions about voting and, as a result, feels more involved in the process.

QUESTION: In earlier discussion the premise seemed to be that the quality of the reading matter does not really make a difference. Any reading may be better than no reading, but the overall quality of our culture stands at risk if we lower the quality of newspapers, for example, to reach those people who do not read.

What kinds of things should be done to entice people to start at the basic level but to demand more substantial content eventually? How can we encourage people to read something of a little better quality than what they are flocking to now?

MS. FOUTZ: The question requires attention, and I do address it in my work with teachers. We compare the content of newspapers from around the country. To cite one specific project, we have an activity we call "target date" in which we send for twenty-five or thirty different newspapers of the same date and compare the content. We examine the papers together, and then the teachers in turn use them in their classrooms. This activity is suitable for junior high or high school students, who are ready to make such comparisons and to recognize the difference between good reporting and slanted or biased reporting. All of these mental processes are part of critical thinking.

QUESTION: How can we raise the level of reading? Many books at a variety of levels of difficulty can be pursued resulting from a "hook," such as the CBS presentation of "All Quiet on the Western Front," or a theme such as a special relationship. I think the job of the educator, then, is to try to build upon the interest of the student in a particular area.

DR. LEVINE: We seem to assume that aliteracy is related to the reading level of the individual, but this assumption is not necessarily the case. Clearly, significant numbers of students with poor skills do avoid reading, but some people who have excellent skills are simply not reading. In my own acquaintance I have a growing number of people who have excellent reading skills and come from a middle- or upper-middle-class socioeconomic background but who have ceased reading newspapers. Reading skills are related to the issue of aliteracy, but I think other factors are involved.

COMMENT: Perhaps because I am with the Literacy Council of Northern Virginia, my viewpoint is way down the scale; I do not have the elitist problem of training people to read the *New York Times* intelligently. Looking at the statistics from the census data, we used to label those with a fourth grade

25

education or less illiterate, or at least functionally illiterate. In the 1960 census from 5 to 10 percent of the population fell into this category. The literacy problem was probably much greater than statistics indicated. The 1980 census data on literacy that are just coming out can probably be thrown into the Potomac River because they show that a very high percentage of people over twenty years of age have now graduated from high school. At our Literacy Council, we find that 10 percent of our illiterate students have high school diplomas. Earlier, the sociologist who commented gave a good indication of reading skills when she observed that her students cannot read rather simple books. As members of the television generation, perhaps they are not able to read books on sociology.

COMMENT: As a newspaperman, I think that you may be giving the content of newspapers rather short shrift. Recently, I was with a group of young people and in the course of the conversation discovered that no one ever read past the jump. They read to the bottom of the column and no further. Now I am a devoted reader of the *New York Times*, but I find nothing on the front page of the *New York Times* that interests me enough to go inside the *New York Times*. The way things are written and presented should be part of this discussion also.

DR. WILSON: The newspaper contains intellectually challenging, stimulating information, and if anything to the contrary has been implied, then it was done unintentionally. I find that the newspaper is one place where the reader is in complete charge. It is a place where the reader is constantly making decisions. The fact that there is not flowing text from one article to the other is an advantage because the reader does not have to read the whole piece: he can make choices. I see that feature as challenging, intellectually challenging.

QUESTION: You don't see it as a barrier? The *New York Times* is interesting to adults, but invariably dull to a young person. As for the *Washington Post*, a reader can find world events on the front page, but very little about the dog that ran away, which is the kind of story that people do like to read.

MR. THIMMESCH: We are referring to the *Washington Post–New York Times* journalism as opposed to Murdoch journalism. Behind the last remark is the conviction that some human interest or other attraction must pull the reader into the story. Both the *New York Times* and the *Post* rather dutifully try to develop background and depth on their stories, creating conflict between the necessity of interesting the readers and the duty of informing them.

COMMENT: Three observations come to mind on issues that have been raised.

First, the sustained silent reading program described earlier has an interesting application in many schools, where not only the students are involved, but also the janitors, cafeteria workers, and principals—in fact, everyone in the school reads for a specific time period everyday. The adults thereby set examples, as readers, for the students.

Second, some very interesting and revealing research has recently come from Indiana University that suggests conclusions contrary to much previous discussion here. Much of this research is identified with Dr. Roger Farr, a past president of the International Reading Association. This research suggests rather convincingly that in the case of elementary children and, to a lesser degree, high school students, students are reading better at comparable grade levels than they were a generation ago. This finding holds true even though a typical third grader today is younger than a typical third grader a generation ago. This study does not measure how much they are reading, but it does compare their capabilities to those of their grade-level peers of a generation ago.

Third, we have not really addressed the issue of whether reading is really necessary or to what extent it is really necessary. Perhaps everyone at the head table and certainly most of the people in this room in one way or another depend on the survival of reading for their livelihoods, as well as for their professional egos and well-being. This fact does not necessarily invalidate their views, but it does suggest a likely bias. We emphasize functional literacy and stress our conviction that everyone needs reading to perform his life roles. Whereas we might like to think that individuals regard voting and being good citizens as part of their necessary life roles, we must realize that these are not the highest priority. The highest priority for most of us is our jobs and our immediate environments. Perhaps we are guilty of suggesting that reading is an essential functional skill for everyone because we have a vested interest in it. I am a reading person, I believe in reading, I have taught illiterates, I have published in this area. I am for furthering literacy, but maybe we are misled. Twenty years ago, I took three years of high school Latin because my role models at the time, my guidance counselors, my parents, and people in a position to influence me assured me that one needed Latin to be a success in the world. No one could explain why knowing Latin was essential—it just was. Perhaps we're guilty of some of that reasoning, and maybe we should consider the question as we discuss this issue.

QUESTION: Two issues need further clarification: flexibility in the reading process and diversity in newspapers. How can we strike a balance between the preference for fairly simple reading material—in newspapers, for example—and the need to handle complex technical materials? How will people handle the difficult material if their regular reading diet is on a much simpler level?

DR. LEVINE: You raise the important question of the costs of easy reading. We should consider that question here, and society as a whole should consider it. As we write our newspapers, textbooks, and other reading material at the level of less able readers, there are costs involved. At some point, an individual may arrive at a point where job requirements as well as the requirements of intelligent political involvement could extend beyond the limits of his reading capacity. This result might be the real cost of easy reading.

QUESTION: Earlier, someone referred to an Orwellian world where the lower income and minority people become television's biggest audience while people who do the reading become the decision makers. Is there evidence that minorities and the poor will be the nonreaders? Do we know that the readers and the nonreaders split along economic and ethnic lines? Further, can we legitimately value the person who reads the "dumbed down" paper less than the person who reads the good, gray *New York Times*? Is there any evidence that the one who reads the *New York Post* votes less often than the one who reads the *New York Times*? Some fundamental assumptions are at issue here. I question the validity of discussing these matters in ethnic, economic, and elitist terms.

MR. THIMMESCH: I think the networks can document that an increasing portion of television viewership is among minority and lower income people. In the inner city, television has almost become a utility; it is turned on in the morning and is often left on all day, becoming a prime source of information and entertainment. Studies also show that people who rely on television to make political decisions and decisions about candidates make their choices subjectively on how the candidate looks or on how effective the commercial is. We all recognize the great tyranny in political advertising today. A candidate can have the strongest logic and the best program, but if the spot commercials are not compelling, that person may not be elected. Perhaps someone will clarify the issue of reading and television use by those in the inner city.

MS. GRASZ: The information that we get strongly supports the claim that those in the inner city are principally television viewers. As an educational telecommunications specialist in one of the few such network-sponsored programs, I know that we are busily trying to increase and improve our outreach and the quality and level of literacy of our programming, but we cannot overlook the fact that our audience consists principally not of readers but of television viewers.

MR. THIMMESCH: Ms. Grasz, haven't I read that CBS has recognized that their future viewership will increasingly come from the minority community and from the inner city community?

MS. GRASZ: The bigger question here concerns what is really happening in this country and of how we are using our time. Basically, people are lazy. They want to get information and entertainment the easiest way that they can. If information can be spoon-fed by radio or with pictures or on television, people will seek it out in that form. Reading does take an effort. People find they have so many restrictions on their personal time that perhaps they consider reading a luxury they have no time for. Maybe vacation is their only chance to read. My job keeps me so busy that I am selective in what I do. The same is happening to everyone else.

In addition, those in a lower income bracket feel that they do not have the money to buy books. Books have gone up in price, a probable explanation for the increased use of libraries.

Earlier, I cited a figure of 41,000 for the number of new books published in this country. The number has actually dropped about 5,000 over the last several years because of the economic situation in this country, time restrictions, and our own laziness.

COMMENT: To clarify a point that was made earlier, I will cite some analyses of typical issues of *Reader's Digest*. The readability level of the articles reflects exactly that of the original source, running anywhere from sixth to twelfth or thirteenth grade level. Thinking is hard work, and reading challenging material is a form of thinking. Reading requires that one interact with the material, setting up a kind of dialogue. Reading requires a level of mental activity, and that's hard work, which people tend to resist.

To make another ancillary point, I suspect that a correlation exists between people who read challenging material and people who are successful. We should devise a way to persuade people who read easy material or who read nothing at all that it is worth the effort to read challenging material and that it may pay off in some unforeseen way.

QUESTION: I have two concerns to raise with the television people, the educators, and the newspaper people. My first concern is with the survival of scientific education in the United States. In one of the recent newspapers, an article claimed that 40 to 50 percent of today's Ph.D.s in scientific areas are from foreign countries. Are foreign countries doing a better job teaching reading than we are? I have almost completed a study of gifted children in Fairfax County. I asked them what they were reading and found that all they read are fiction and sports. They do not read in the sciences, they do not read in anthropology. They have never read anything but sports and fiction. This small range of reading limits these young people because the structure of the sentences in each discipline is different. A biology text differs from an English literature text. Mathematicians use a distinctive language structure. If children are not exposed to these differences when they are rather young, they may

29

be excluded from those fields. Somewhere along the line, we in education, those of you in the newspaper business, and those of you in television are not giving our children the structure of the language in the disciplines where the jobs will be in the future. We are shutting out the children from the inner city from certain fields because they have never been exposed to the language. They will not acquire sufficient exposure through television.

Maybe television eventually could teach the patterns of the language of these disciplines. In general, they will not gain what they need from newspapers, either. Some of the more intellectually sophisticated newspapers provide some of the necessary breadth, but the sciences are inadequately represented. What are we doing, then, to keep this scientific world of ours going, and what are we doing to educate our children in the thinking patterns of the job market?

DR. LEVINE: You have articulated very well one of the costs of easy reading that I had in the back of my mind earlier. On a positive note, we can look forward to even greater and more sophisticated use of technology in the classroom that will address just this kind of issue. A whole new area that we have hardly touched on in our discussion is the use of technology in the education process and its effect on reading. Technology may already have the capacity to identify and develop those differences in language patterns specific to various disciplines that were just noted. If the technology does not yet exist, it clearly will.

QUESTION: Could someone comment on the direction of this conference and on the ideas on which we should focus?

DR. LEVINE: I presented this group with three important objectives in considering the question of aliteracy. The first was to identify whether the problem exists and, if so, to what degree the problem exists, and what its nature is. Clearly, we need to know about the problem in more detail. The second point is the question of whether reading makes a difference, whether it has a value, and if it is something to be greatly valued. Many people have commented on that issue. More can certainly be said about it. The third area, which concerns what can be done about aliteracy, remains open.

MR. THIMMESCH: Our exploration of aliteracy will now focus more on books and magazines, rather than on newspapers. Television, of course, will figure in this discussion; with 77 million American homes with television sets today and 30 percent of these wired for cable television, we are on the threshold of an expanding era of telecommunications.

Literacy has been long valued as a boon to humanity, and perhaps we are even somewhat dogmatic about it; but simple illiteracy is no longer a significant problem. The affliction of total illiteracy is all but wiped out in our country. The real problem is aliteracy because if people fail to use the rational process demanded by reading, what kind of decisions are they going to make for themselves and society?

I recall that when that Brahmin of syndicated columnists, Joseph Alsop, quit writing, he explained in great lament that the printed word was doomed, so why should he go on? Leon Botstein, the young president of Bard College, sees an aliteracy crisis among the supposedly well-educated and says that even the best students today arrive at college unable to express their ideas on paper. Indeed, a writer for the *Los Angeles Times* reported that publishers are "dumbing down" the college textbooks because today's students cannot handle difficult material. Some anomalies, however, should be noted in the world of books and magazines. Library use is up while the retail hardcover book business is not doing very well. The magazine industry reports that it is healthy and that its circulation has grown nearly twice as fast in the past thirty years as the population. Before we blame the decline of book and newspaper reading on television, we should remember that the startling bestseller, *Why Johnny Can't Read*, appeared in 1955, several years before the majority of American homes had television sets. Then again, scores on the scholastic aptitude tests have shown a steady decline from the time the first television generation of young people began applying to college in the early 1960s. The next several papers will introduce fresh thought on the state of reading today: Is reading really declining as a skill among the majority of Americans, or are we fretting too much about it or ignoring the educative qualities of video communications?

Books in an Electronic Age

John Y. Cole

I will approach the issue of television and the influence of the electronic society on books, on libraries, and on reading, by describing very briefly the organization I represent: the Center for the Book in the Library of Congress.

Center for the Book

Our center was created in 1977 on the assumption that in this electronic age, it is essential that we continually remind ourselves and our citizens of the importance of books and reading to our civilization. What is different about this organization is that it was established within the Library of Congress by Daniel J. Boorstin, the Librarian of Congress, expressly to keep the book flourishing in a society increasingly dominated by information rather than by knowledge. Although our center draws on the resources of the Library of Congress, we work primarily with organizations outside the Library of Congress, with publishing, educational, and other organizations throughout the United States to do the following. First, we try to heighten the public's awareness of books, and we do this largely by using other media. Up to now, we have relied primarily on television to promote books and reading. Second, we try to stimulate the study of books and reading. Third, we encourage the international flow of books and other printed materials. Fourth, we work to improve the quality of book production.

While our major concern naturally is the book, we define book in a rather inclusive way, describing our overall goal as promoting books, reading, and the printed word. We operate by bringing together members of the book, educational, and business communities for symposia and for projects. We also sponsor lectures and publications and hope to begin sponsoring more exhibits and perhaps a film or two before long. Our organization tries to serve as a catalyst and, true to its catalytic function, it has a full-time staff of only two people. The Library of Congress provides administrative support; our programs, projects, and publications are paid for by tax-deductible contributions from individuals and organizations. In this sense, the center is a unique partnership between the government and the private sector. In fact, when the center was established, a special law was passed that enabled it to use private contributions for its operations.

Support for the Center

I am happy to report that fiscally we are in good shape. During the past year, our center has received contributions from thirty individuals and thirty-five corporations, most of whom are publishers, and we are grateful to the publishing community for this support. We also have received support in relatively small sums from foundations. Our center requires only about $100,000 a year to operate, which is not much. We are fortunate in having support from a variety of sources; we like to get many small contributions because this involves more frequent exchanges between our center and outside organizations. We rely on outside ideas, and more than that, we rely on other organizations to take our ideas and implement them into their own programs. We simply are not large enough to run any big operations.

Programs at the Center

Reading and literacy naturally are two of our major interests. Our publications and other projects mirror this interest. "Television, the Book and the Classroom" was our first symposium; "Read More about It," referred to in an earlier paper, is a project that grew out of a symposium. It is now jointly sponsored by the Library of Congress and CBS Television. A symposium we held in 1978 on "Reading in America" incorporated the book industry study group's major survey of reading habits in America, which is frequently cited in support of this or that observation about reading habits, but usually showing great alarm at what is happening to reading in America. "The Textbook in American Society" is an examination of the textbook and its role; this symposium attracted mostly textbook publishers and textbook authors, but we also raised other issues such as censorship. Other publications include "The Book," by Barbara Tuchman, one of our lecturers; "The Audience for the Children's Books"; and our most recent publication called, appropriately enough, "A Nation of Readers," which is an address given by Daniel Boorstin about the importance of books and reading in American life.

We have also mounted several campaigns to promote reading. "Read More about It" with CBS Television is an example. We are now working with the national PTA, the International Reading Association, and the National Association of School Administrators. We work mostly through other groups and organizations following up on a major national conference we had on "The Family-School Partnership in Encouraging Reading." This event took place last November, and we are still working with these organizations on the subject. We have a "Books Make a Difference" project, which was an oral history interview project that now is crystallizing very nicely; one of the results will be a national contest for students this fall sponsored by Xerox Educational Publications whereby students, in their *Weekly Reader* and *Read* magazines, will be encouraged to write 200-word essays about how books or something that they read has made a difference in their lives and what that difference was. This will be a national contest and the student winners selected by Xerox will be brought to Washington, D.C., for a tour of Washington and, of course, for a visit to the Library of Congress. Next spring, we will publish a book titled *Literacy and Historical Perspective*, based on a recent conference. We also play the role of host for many organizations concerned with reading and literacy. Last Wednesday, for example, we were the host for the U.S. celebration of International Literacy Day. Mrs. George Bush, the Secretary of Education, and a number of other officials came to talk about literacy programs in the United States and to celebrate the progress of International Literacy Day.

Importance of Books and Reading

Philosophically, we would agree that there is an aliteracy problem based just on the direction that our program has taken. Our emphasis, for example, has been on promoting reading to people who can read already. We have, of course, been involved in some other kinds of literacy programs, but thus far, our emphasis has been on reaching adult readers and reminding them of the value of books and reading and on promoting the reading of books however we can. In our symposia, lectures, and publications, in our announcements after television programs, and in articles in the popular press, members of our National Advisory Board, especially Daniel Boorstin, remind people of the difference between the information bombarding them from all directions through the media and the knowledge available only through reading books. This knowledge is contained in those unique institutions of knowledge called libraries and schools that our society, perhaps, seems to be on the verge of neglecting. Dr. Boorstin has elaborated this theme several times in the popular press, for example, in *TV Guide* earlier this year and this month in an article in *Reader's Digest*. In the *Reader's Digest* article, he reminds us that books continue to be the catalyst and incentive for much of the knowledge of the human race and, again, that there is a basic difference between a well but superficially informed citizenry and a knowledgeable citizenry. In her lecture for us, Barbara Tuchman called books the "carriers of civilization" and "humanity in print," two especially apposite phrases that we use frequently in our promotional literature.

The Library of Congress has become involved in this effort to help organize, focus, and dramatize our nation's interest in books and reading because we share the concern of those at this meeting about the future of reading in our country and feel that, as the national library, we have a special reason to see that books do not go unread and that they are read by people of all ages and conditions.

Aliteracy and the Decline of the Language

Townsend Hoopes

I will try to address the question posed by the title of the conference, which seems somewhat loaded. There's not a great deal of hard evidence on either side of the literacy point, despite Mark Russell's dictum that one in every five Americans is illiterate, not including the moral majority. What, one may fairly ask, do the planners of this seminar mean by the decision-making process—personal, family, corporate, national, global? Taking the question as posed, I would say, broadly, yes, the decision-making process is endangered. An intelligent—certainly a wide—public participation in the political decision-making process is jeopardized by a decline of reading among what are thought to be our educated classes.

The Consequences of Semiliteracy

Why is this decline a danger? I am convinced that there is an inextricable connection between a failure to read and an inability to write and that this deterioration produces a semiliteracy, which in turn leads to a genuine breakdown in communications. An ability to write clearly has always been a reflection of an ability to think clearly, but clear thinking is greatly facilitated by, if not absolutely dependent upon, the ability to use the tested tools of precise words and established meanings encased in a coherent sentence structure. Our regard for the structure of language is what concerns me most. Our use of the language has become so debased that it is destroying the ability even of educated people to evaluate ideas clearly and to communicate their views to others. We are plagued everyday by hordes of teenagers and now post-teenagers who seem reasonably proficient orally, but who do not in fact speak in sentences. If one listens carefully, he will observe that their speech is unstructured, fragmented, impressionistic. They lack both the precision and the power of succinct generalization. They use phrases without content,

36

like getting "your act together," which is a pathetic shorthand substitute for thinking through and saying what they mean. Their talk is endlessly interlarded with "like" and "you know," which are desperate attempts to fill up the empty spaces in the brain and link together those incoherent fragments that float in the void. This phenomenon is genuine semiliteracy, and I think it is a blight upon the language and upon intelligent communication. In my judgment, it is full justification for strangulation or perhaps defenestration from the second floor.

The Causes of Semiliteracy

One must acknowledge that the people who can read but won't are to some extent shaped by the same general environment that is producing widespread functional illiteracy, as we now define it, because it is a process that feeds on itself, producing a pernicious downward spiral. A failure of the schools to insist on high standards of reading, writing, and spelling leads to a decline in all of these. This state, in turn, leads to a lowering of academic requirements because the majority of students cannot meet the old ones. Most important, the decline produces in the second and succeeding generations a crop of English teachers who are clearly substandard, not well-grounded in even the fundamentals of grammar and not remotely well-read. The students of such teachers, be they smart or dumb, are bound to be handicapped. We are dealing here with a contagious virus, a literal application of Gresham's law that bad coinage drives out good.

The Effect on National Affairs

What is the effect of all these forces on the future for responsible citizen participation in our national affairs? Last year one federally supported research organization reported results that are hardly surprising—that teenagers read very little for their own enjoyment, spend more time watching television than they spend reading, and prefer movies to books. The inevitable consequence, said this organization, is that these children are satisfied with their initial and almost always shallow interpretations of what they do read and deeply resist requests or instructions to explain or defend their points of view with reasoned analysis or cogency. The "me" generation seems to believe that a purely subjective opinion is valid. The same research organization concluded that "many students believe they will emerge from school into an electronic world that will require little reading and less writing. Nothing could be further from the truth. In a world overloaded with information, both a business and a personal advantage will go to those individuals who can sort the wheat from the chaff. A society in which the habits of disciplined reading, analysis, interpretation, and discourse are not sufficiently cultivated has much to fear."

It is a fact that less than a majority of Americans read books with any regularity, and that less than 25 percent are moderate to heavy readers (defined as ten to thirty or more books a year). It is also a fact that these latter are the leadership groups, conscious of the superior educational and informational value of books over magazines and newspapers (though they do read such publications and also watch TV). This latter fact seems, at first glance, to run against the general perception that television and poor schools are steadily eroding our national reading habits and turning us into passive boob tube zombies. At least a substantial fraction of the population is reading a great deal, and serious stuff. But we may be witnessing a widening gap between the leadership elites and the general public. The engaged, energetic, and motivated leadership groups are reading serious books, thereby reinforcing their power and influence, while the mass public is sinking into a passive contentment with soaps and sitcoms.

To keep the moderate perspective, however, we should acknowledge that things may not be as bad as they seem or at least not very different from what they have been. Serious book reading has never become an ingrained habit outside the highly motivated leadership groups in any society, and the influence of those groups has always been considerably disproportionate to their size. People today may not be reading fewer books; it may be that they are reading more books. Until the last year or two in fact, more new titles have been published every year for the last decade or two. Perhaps a substitution is occurring, though. Formula books, for example, like the Harlequin and Candlelight Romances, which are selling like hot cakes, are really a substitute for the old magazines like *True Confessions*, which are now defunct. Similarly, instant paperback books covering some topical and dramatic event like *The Raid at Entebbe* are filling the gap left by the demise of *Life Magazine*, *Collier's*, and *The Saturday Evening Post*.

The Gap between Reality and Expectations

In a real sense, the scope of the problem may lie in the gap between our expectations for universal intellectual equality in a democracy and the colder reality. During World War I, a vast number of young Americans were drafted into the army who could barely write more than their own name. The country made soldiers of them and declined to call them illiterate. After World War II, we embraced the assumption that almost everyone is capable of a college education and can benefit from it. That assumption has suffered some rude shocks in recent years on both intellectual and financial grounds.

To sum up, I believe it is the threatened debasement of language that is at the root of our justifiable alarm, for this debasement impairs the ability to understand, to reason, to analyze, and to communicate. This impairment presents the greatest danger for a democratic system. In a world of increasing social, economic, and technical complexity, power will almost inevitably devolve upon those with the greatest knowledge. If the gap between the educated minority and the undereducated mass becomes too great, the opportunities for political manipulation will grow, and the philosophical underpinnings of our political system will be open to serious question.

The Magazine Industry in a Time of Change

Kent Rhodes

Every time a new communications medium arrives on the scene, people seem to think magazines are doomed. That was true when radio came along, and it was true when television came along. True to form, there is now speculation about cable television and the demise of the magazine. Just the opposite has occurred over the years. Magazines have faced these new communications media, and they are alive and well today. True, we have seen the demise of *The Saturday Evening Post* and the old *Life*, though there is a new *Life* now. Other magazines come along and pick up just as much readership as those magazines had in their heyday.

Is Aliteracy a Problem?

I had never heard of aliteracy until I was invited to present my views on the subject. I am not convinced that there is any such thing that we should be worried about. Consequently, I will not address the question of whether the decision-making process is in danger. I think it is always endangered, but I question whether it is in any more danger now than it ever has been. Certainly, I think magazines are contributing to a constructive elimination of aliteracy.

The health of the magazine industry depends on reading. We could not survive unless people liked to read and liked to buy magazines, and they are buying more magazines than they ever bought before. Magazine circulation is up 92 percent in the last thirty years. During that period the adult population went up only 55 percent. Yet, the cost to the reader of the average magazine is now about $1.68 per single copy, three times its price in 1973. Nine out of every ten adults in our surveys read at least one magazine a month, and the average person reads eight magazines a month. The number of magazines with a circulation of a million per issue has increased: There were forty-nine in 1966, and there are sixty-three of them now. From an economic point of view the magazine industry now derives more of its income than it used to from circulation, that is, from readers. Previously, about one-third came from readers and two-thirds from advertisers whereas now it is almost fifty-fifty. This is a clear indication that people are willing to pay more for their reading material.

A Thriving Magazine Industry

In her paper Lynne Grasz of CBS singled out the *National Enquirer* and the celebrity-oriented magazines as typical popular publications and contrasted them with news, the hot item on television. She referred to *Sixty Minutes* as a mini-documentary. First, we should observe that *Sixty Minutes* is in a magazine format (we're rather complimented by that); second, *Time*, *Newsweek*, and *U.S. News & World Report*, the leading news magazines of the country, have never enjoyed such large circulations as they have today. The circulation of *Time* is now 4.3 million copies an issue. Not so long ago it was 2 million copies an issue. People are interested in news, and I maintain that a great many of them are getting their news from magazines.

In addition to the flourishing news magazines, other well-established magazines are doing quite well. The *Reader's Digest* has a circulation of 17 million copies an issue; *TV Guide* has the next largest circulation; the third highest is the *National Geographic* with 10.8 million copies per issue. Not long ago, around 1965, the *National Geographic* circulated only 5 million copies an issue.

Changing Tastes

Now many new magazines serve all kinds of specific interests, whether the readers be congressmen, businessmen, travelers, lawyers, doctors, intellectuals, high-flyers, skin divers, gardeners—we have a magazine for all of them. Magazines are continuing to serve and fill the important needs of the consumer public. Change is an everyday occurrence in the marketplace; as consumer tastes and needs and interests and behavior have changed, magazines have changed. For confirmation of these changes, all we have to do is examine magazines published ten years ago and look at the changes. Magazines are dynamic; editors are dynamic. Their presentations are different from what they used to be; color, typography, and format are different; new words are in vogue.

We in the industry think we are encouraging people to read, and we know that they are certainly buying more magazines. A cynic might observe that to buy is not necessarily to read, but a magazine cannot survive that way very long.

41

Education and Affluence

Two factors promote the growth of the magazine industry, the first of which is education. We find a very definite correlation between magazine reading and education. The more education people have, the more they read magazines. The second factor is affluence: The more money people have, the more they spend on magazines. Studies for our advertisers show clearly that the more people read, the less they view television. The wealthier people are, the more time they spend reading; the more educated they are, the more time they spend reading. Because both affluence and education are increasing in this country, we view the future as a coming boom.

A skeptic might ask how we define reading. The answers are not conclusive regarding magazine reading. In some of the surveys people are asked if they recall seeing an article and if they have read it. On that basis, the average magazine has about four and a half readers. Those survey techniques show our audience to be just as great as the television audience. The television audience is defined by the number of sets turned on, not by the number of those looking at them. We are keeping up with television, then.

Skills at Play in Magazine Reading

In his paper, Dr. Wilson referred to his expectations concerning articles in the newspaper; he anticipated being challenged and forced to use critical skills and thinking skills to search out the information that he wanted in the newspaper. He pointed out that a reader chooses articles. The reader does the same in a magazine. He goes through it and chooses what he wants to read; he is an active reader, and an active reader gets a great deal more out of this presentation of information than he will ever get on television.

These comments come from my conviction that television is not, in fact, sweeping away the need for reading. Reading is a highly personal act in which the reader is completely engrossed in a subject that he or she wants to know more about. I contend that magazines are storehouses of knowledge, and I submit that if a person wants the most current news, the most recent analysis, he will find what he needs in magazines because the most up-to-date information is too new for books. I am impressed with the ability of magazines to focus on things that their particular segment of the reading audience wants, and certainly newspapers are beginning to provide special formats to display certain news items for their audiences. In this respect, newspapers and magazines have greater capability than the broadcast media because the readership knows the publication and would not buy it otherwise. For in-depth information, I cite just one article—William Greider's piece on David Stockman in the *Atlantic Monthly*. Where else could it have been found?

The Role of the Schools in the Teaching of Reading

Vincent Reed

Although I do not wish to exclude the family, I will emphasize the role of the school in the teaching of reading.

Decreasing Support for Education

In this country, we have 16,000 school districts; in those 16,000 school districts, we have 41 million elementary and secondary school children. The year before last, this country spent $118 billion educating students in kindergarten through twelfth grade. I had an opportunity last year in the Department of Education to move around the country. As I did, I heard concern expressed that the communities are having difficulty justifying the large amounts of money needed to educate our students and to support school systems. I began to ask why, given that education is the basis of our society, there is such resistance to funding public education.

I got a variety of answers, but one seemed to be the thread throughout. People are disillusioned when they see that so many of our young people graduating from the twelfth grade cannot function at the twelfth-grade level. Extensive research as well as simple observation indicates that we have too many youngsters coming out of our schools who cannot function at the level that they are given credit for. In answer to these critics, I agreed that if one student with a high school diploma is unable to function at the twelfth-grade level, that is too many. I reminded them, though, that certainly not all youngsters who come out of public schools are unable to function. I rejected that misconception because I know better. How do you account, they then ask, for the research that tells us that one out of every ten graduating seniors from high school last year could not perform the most elementary reading tasks? How do you account for the fourteen-year decline in SAT scores, forty-nine points on the verbal component and thirty-two points on the math? What about the 3 million in this country who cannot read the daily newspaper?

Now last year when I heard that last question, I was not so concerned; but since I have been with the *Washington Post*, I am really worried because 3 million people in this country will not buy a newspaper because they cannot read! I pointed out to these critics that whatever is happening to education has been going on over a long period. They complained that education today has lost its focus on achievement and that educators are primarily concerned about keeping youngsters in school and moving them along, and then they graduate them without having imparted the basic skills.

Remedial Actions

At the time I became superintendent, I had to ask myself that question—why is it that so many of our young people are not achieving? We found out that the first thing we had to do was to make an assessment of our situation. In this period of evaluation we found that because many of our young people had not developed the skills early in the prekindergarten and continued progressing through the twelfth grade, they were not achieving. We then set up the programs that would go about the business of developing skills; we also abolished social promotions and imposed standards. Most are familiar with social promotions: that is, promotion of youngsters based on age and maturity rather than on academic achievement and classroom performance. We set the standards that would require young people to read. We found that we had been *teaching* reading but not *mandating* reading. We taught youngsters how to read but did not demand achievement of the goal.

At that point we had to develop ways to make youngsters read after they had been given the fundamentals and the techniques of reading. We did several things. We started a program called "Portal to Portal Reading" in junior high schools, where everybody had to carry a book—every teacher had to be seen with a book all day long, every student had to carry a book, and we imposed certain penalties for not having a book. For fifteen minutes every morning, everybody stopped everything regardless of the discipline and read for fifteen minutes. Nobody prescribed what the students read, but every classroom teacher had to see that the students did read something. We instituted two fifteen-minute reading periods, one in the morning and one in the afternoon, to make sure everybody read fifteen minutes during the day. If we fail to start youngsters reading at this level, then the chances of catching up with it later are almost nil.

Reading and Real Comprehension

Another phenomenon we found is that while we were teaching youngsters to read, we were not teaching youngsters to comprehend. The youngsters had learned to call words to get past the classroom situation, but they had not really absorbed the meaning of what they had read. I went into a classroom once where the teacher was bragging about how well these youngsters read in second grade—and they were reading. It amazed me how well they ran through the words. When a youngster turned to the next page, though, I put a piece of paper over the picture at the top: The youngster could not read a word on that page. The students had simply memorized the text, taking cues from the illustrations, but to all appearances, reading. We had to go back to make sure that the students comprehended. Once youngsters read and understood what they read, we found them reading and looking forward to reading for information and for the other satisfactions that motivate them.

Reading and Television

As we got into the whole issue of electronic media, we were constantly criticized by the claims of some in the community that too many youngsters spent too much time before the television set. My position was that because we could not control parents and order them to turn off the television set, we should use electronic media to support what we were doing. As a result, we explored with CBS ways that the network could help us teach youngsters to read. From New York they shipped us thousands of copies of forthcoming shows like "Little House on the Prairie" so that our students could read the scripts prior to the show. Then when the show was aired, they knew the story, and the next day we discussed it in the classroom. We attracted criticism, particularly from the Board of Education, which indicated its disapproval of our encouraging youngsters to watch television. I was convinced, though, that because television is going to prevail, we should use it to reinforce our efforts. We established several of these programs to make reading a priority and to encourage youngsters to read once we had taught them to read.

Reading is the business of the school, and the school must make sure that youngsters have in their hands the material to read and that reading will take place.

Success in Reading

During the time that I was in the school system, the *Washington Post* began and has continued a program called "Success in Reading," where teachers are trained to use the newspaper in teaching elementary and junior high school children how to read. Not only do they teach youngsters how to read by using the newspaper, but also they teach math with the newspaper. We just finished a program this past August, training teachers anew to use the newspaper in teaching students how to read. We have to explore every way that we can to encourage children to read, to let them know that reading is important in their lives, and to convince them that someday this skill may be of benefit to them.

Those who have engaged themselves in the educational process know that one of the hardest things is to make youngsters understand that what they are doing today will mean something to them ten years or fifteen years from now. Once they understand that, we have taken the first step toward motivating them to read.

Books Are Essential

Of course, we have to make sure that books are available. We have to make sure that magazines are available. When we cut budgets, we cannot cut book orders and magazine subscriptions. We must understand that some things are more important in the school system than those teachers in the classroom. I used to hear all the time that if dollars must be cut from the budget, cut everything but classroom teachers. Some people assert that if we have nothing but kids in a classroom and a teacher is present, then we have solved the problem. I say that there is more to teaching youngsters how to read than having a classroom teacher. Classroom teachers are important, but a classroom teacher without the support to encourage youngsters to do certain things is of no avail. School systems will really have to bite the bullet more or less.

Setting Standards

Superintendents must set standards; they must set standards themselves to teach youngsters how to read and must involve parents in the process.

As for social promotions, for years I have been assured that flunking is psychologically damaging to students. What is the result of this philosophy? We have passed them right along to make everybody happy. Nobody is angry, parents are happy, youngsters pass. Parents do not come to school when youngsters pass; parents come to school when youngsters fail. Failing a student is not the best way to get parents to see the teacher or the principal, but when you become as desperate as we all have been in the past, we will use any methods possible to get them into school. Very few parents will question the substance of a passing grade, but very few parents will not stop in the school to find out why a youngster failed. If you set standards and maintain those standards, then students will have to read to meet those standards.

Many opportunities will open to resourceful educators and parents as they enlist in dedicated efforts to teach children the skills of reading at the same time they communicate the urgent necessity.

Discussion

DR. LEVINE: Mr. Cole and Mr. Hoopes both raised questions about the impact of the information age on this requirement for literacy. The impact of the information age brings with it both threat and a requirement for literacy. Mr. Cole drew the distinction between information and knowledge, and Mr. Hoopes referred to the requirement that we be able to sort through and process the information that is presented, which in itself is a literacy requirement. An expansion on the definition of literacy in that context might be useful.

MR. HOOPES: Clearly, a dramatic transformation will occur in the form of books over the next ten or twenty years. We will probably see, for example, computer-based encyclopedias. We are already seeing television and computer-assisted complements to textbooks, a trend that is likely to increase. The computer software now being used as an aid to education is really in its infancy. We now appear to have solved one basic problem: whether there would be enough computers out there in the population to take the software that can assist and supplement textbooks. The answer is now clearly affirmative. Many microcomputers are coming in at a cost within the range of most institutions and some families. I foresee an explosive growth of educational business as well as expanded personal uses for information conveyed through software cassettes and discs and tapes.

In another realm of book publishing, in what we call professional publishing, the scientific, technical, and medical books contain, to some extent, time-urgent information. The researchers, the people who are on the frontiers of knowledge, use this information and they want it promptly. We are already seeing, of course, a larger volume of information of that sort conveyed by computer or a variety of computer and television technology. In the first instance we will see it in two forms. Publishers will publish hard copy in book form, and they will simultaneously make the information available to people who would like access to it in computers. Undeniably, television and the computer have become a fundamental part of the technology of our era. As Dr. Reed noted, since we cannot beat it, we really must use it and adjust to it. I see us in the infancy of our constructive adjustments to these revolutionary new techniques.

COMMENT: The computer literacy programs springing up all over the country are good because for the first time our interest in technology has moved from the theoretical level to the classroom where youngsters can get practical, hands-on experience. The computer seems to be a strong motivation for young people. They are intrigued by the computer, and these programs have many by-products, increased attendance, for example. Computer training is important, not only as a preparation for future jobs, but also as a means for students to realize their potential.

QUESTION: Mr. Rhodes, although you began your presentation by saying you did not feel that there was a problem with lack of reading, you later said that you saw a positive correlation between higher education and higher affluence and magazine consumption. I realize that you are looking at this issue from a marketing perspective, but those educators who work with people without higher education and affluence might see a problem here. Do you?

MR. RHODES: Certainly. I was only trying to say that the problem is not a new one and that I think all of us in the magazine world would like to do everything we can, not only for the less educated or well off, but also for those who are functionally illiterate. I regret that we do not have a program under way of the kind that CBS has. We have been supportive of "Reading Is Fundamental" over the years. We have other things under consideration at the moment, but we do find it hard as an industry to do more than to call attention in our own magazines to the problem that you just mentioned. The power of magazines really is editorial power, and to supplement that, the Advertising Council is now studying a campaign to address functional illiteracy. We have been working with the council on that program, along with the American Library Association and others.

QUESTION: Mr. Hoopes, what do you see as a solution to the problem you described as a widening gap between the educated minority and uneducated mass as the information society advances? Some people have suggested, for example, that the discrepancies may disappear as information becomes more readily available through the various technological means.

MR. HOOPES: Do you mean that the problem of educational and intellectual inequality will disappear? I doubt it very much. The mass availability of more raw information is not education per se. One wonders, for example, whether the proliferation of cable television channels is really going to make a qualitative improvement in television fare. It certainly is going to pour forth substantially more information, much of it duplicative. That increase does not constitute education in the sense meant by either Mr. Reed or me. There is something altogether too passive about the intake of information from television to constitute the active workings of a mind.

QUESTION: Would you suggest a solution?

MR. HOOPES: I am not sure there is a solution in the present context. What I did say in my paper was that if the gap between the educated minority and the uneducated mass becomes too great, then the opportunities for political manipulation will grow. To find the lesson, we simply have to look back at the history of other countries where tyrannical minorities have manipulated the majorities. I devoutly hope it does not happen here, but it seems to me that one must face up to that remote possibility if this gap continues to grow.

QUESTION: Mr. Hoopes, you seem to think there is a problem of aliteracy while Mr. Rhodes does not see one. There seems to be a difference of opinion. Could you comment?

MR. HOOPES: I think that there are people today who can read but do not read very much. It seems to me that the trend is accelerating among the younger generation, and I find this a matter of some despair.

QUESTION: Mr. Rhodes, you answered the fundamental question of this conference from the point of view of a man in the magazine business who looks forward to boom times ahead. If you look at other print media, for example, can you still affirm your theory that there really is not a problem here?

MR. RHODES: You have to prove to me that there is a problem here. I do not think so. There have been many people who could read in this country but who have not done much reading. I think there are more people able to read by anybody's definition right now in this country than there used to be. Nobody has come up with any real information today to prove what Mr. Hoopes just said, for example, that the younger generation seems to be reading less. I have not seen any such figures, and even if I did, I would suppose that a survey showing contrary results could be found.

COMMENT: The only evidence given to us that could be quantified was the fact that newspaper circulation has been stable while the population has been increasing. There is a pretty strong opinion, I think probably well-reasoned on the part of the newspaper people, that young people were not coming on board as newspaper readers. I think that is the only evidence we have seen so far, and yet you are the only person who has not leapt from that one bit of evidence to the conclusion that we have a problem.

MR. RHODES: Let me make two points. If there are surveys that show that young people are behind the lack of a substantial increase in newspaper circulation, I haven't seen it. I would point out that the cost of newspapers has gone up a great deal more than the cost of magazines. At thirty cents a day the *New York Times* costs $1.80 a week; with the Sunday edition at $1.00, the total is $2.80 a week. I know a lot of young people who would rather buy a copy of *Time* for $1.00 or less or who may turn on the television for nothing. Even if daily newspaper circulation has leveled off at 61 million copies, that is a lot of copies of newspapers—it is millions of words. The daily newspapers supplemented by weekly newspapers and the increasingly popular suburban newspapers provide a lot of reading. I am not convinced that there is a real aliteracy problem here.

QUESTION: I have a long-time interest in these questions on education because I have been teaching for some ten years at the college level. We have noted a potential danger that we will develop two increasingly separate societies. On the one side will be the illiterates and the aliterates, including the social basement; on the other side will be the elite with the cognitive discipline to confront a string of words on paper and to construe and extrapolate from that string of words the range of meaning that the words carry. These people will be the literate people who can make complex distinctions verbally explicit, who can process scientific information and appreciate the complexities of questions like the validity of an interpretation of a proposition and so on. Our society rests on science and technology and relies on people who can use them; we need these elites who can indeed process the written word at effective levels.

Are you claiming that our society will resemble a sandbox in which a lot of people will be playing and building dream castles in the sand but that the sand and the sandbox will belong to somebody else? In other words, is our society developing in such a way that many people will settle into the specious comfort of becoming spectators in their own lives, without effective control over decisions that affect them?

Perhaps literacy is also a power question. As we give consideration to civil rights issues and minority aspirations to rise on the social ladder and to exercise power over their own affairs, can we believe that any such realization of minority hopes is possible without literacy in these groups? Would you agree with this?

COMMENT: There is a feeling with minorities, particularly blacks, that no matter how literate a person is, he will never have decision-making power in this country. The issue goes beyond a simple question of literacy.

QUESTION: In other words, would you say that literacy is perhaps necessary but not sufficient?

COMMENT: Not sufficient to overcome the other ills of this society. Of course, literacy is necessary. With literacy, a person may at least approach the table; whether he can eat once he gets there remains to be seen.

QUESTION: Is literacy something we value just for its own sake, then, rather than for its political implications?

COMMENT: No, literacy is important because when political change becomes possible, a person must be prepared to partake of it. If that person continues to play in that sandbox and gets no further than that, when the opportunity comes, he will not be able to take advantage of it.

QUESTION: Mr. Hoopes, as a publisher of textbooks, could you comment on the pervasiveness of the simplification of language in textbooks in general and on the elimination of reading from science and math books to make them more salable? Also, could you comment on the trends in sales of textbooks? Although I realize there are other factors like the economy and declining enrollment that should be considered, still the sale of textbooks probably is some measure of literacy.

MR. HOOPES: The simplification of texts is a phenomenon, but it is not a recent phenomenon. It has probably been going on for the better part of the last fifteen or twenty years. It may have accelerated in the last decade, but I have no real proof of that. This simplification is a gradual adjustment by the publishers and the educational system to the capacity of the students who enter the schools.

As for recent school textbook sales, they have been quite strong until the last year. They are turning down now as you suggested as a result of the combination of the recession and the demographics. They probably will decline or remain flat for the next few years as Dr. Reed will know better than I.

QUESTION: Dr. Reed, you gave many examples of excellent strategies to improve the reading level of children of low-income and undereducated parents; do you have similar suggestions of ways to improve the reading level of the parents?

DR. REED: We did try to deal with that problem, recognizing that it was a problem. In one instance, we hired a company out of Chicago to set up a reading program through public housing as a joint venture between the public schools and the city government. We intended to go into the public housing complexes and to teach reading to parents as well as to train parents how to assist youngsters with homework. Needless to say, it was not a very successful program. Because so many of the homes had one-parent families, the working hours presented real obstacles.

A more successful program is our adult education program in the public schools. Many adults began attending class during the day in regular high schools. Their presence had a profound effect on several things. The fact that we had adults sitting in classrooms with high school students became a stabilizing factor for many of our high school students. We also found that many parents who needed to be educated and who wanted to further their education could not attend classes at night because they could not afford to pay a babysitter to care for their youngsters at home. We allowed them to go to school during the day. When I left the school system, I had forty-odd adults attending daytime classes in regular high schools. I would like to have gotten more. With some imagination, much can be done. With the decreased enrollment in every urban setting that I know, we should make a strong case for allowing parents to go to school during the day. I see no conflict there at all. If we could get parents into schools during the day, we could set up those programs to deal with their needs and carry them right along with the others. If we enhance the opportunity for parents to participate in the educational process, we improve the advancement of their youngsters.

QUESTION: Mr. Hoopes, in previous discussion the question arose whether reading anything was better than reading nothing, and we briefly addressed the quality of the products on the market. Are you concerned about the quality of today's best sellers? Should we be concerned about the overall quality of reading that people are doing? How can we entice them to read material of higher quality so that the gap between the literate and the aliterate might be lessened?

MR. HOOPES: Let me try to give you an answer from two perspectives. In fairness I ought to stake out a defensible position for Mr. Rhodes and me. Publishers are not social engineers per se. We are in the business of conveying information and literature holding the basic assumption that there is a very large reading public out there. It would impose upon publishers a quite new task if we had to assist in the creation and the nurture of a reading public— in other words, if we were launched directly and explicitly into the business of literacy and education, which has traditionally lain with the schools. From that perspective, I think any reading is better than no reading, and I take no position on best sellers as opposed to esoteric books. I think they both have their place and the more, the better.

If we question the effect of aliteracy on the political decision-making process, then I must speak as a citizen and not as a publisher. As a citizen, I am concerned about the question of quality, about the capacity for interpretation, and about the analytical ability of people who do not read but who spend most of their time playing video games.

QUESTION: Why does there seem to be an enthusiasm in young children for reading and books, and an improvement in the young children in their schools, and yet, by the time they graduate from high school, there seems to be a decline in both improvement levels and interest? What is happening?

COMMENT: Your observation is accurate, and it holds true across the country. Youngsters coming into kindergarten and first grade seem to do very well and to have the enthusiasm and the ability to grasp what is taking place. A decline, though, starts at the third grade. If I knew exactly why, I would be somewhere in the islands enjoying the money I had made.

One explanation might be that through sheer numbers, we throttle the enthusiasm of some youngsters with high pupil-teacher ratios. Even children who are strongly motivated and energetic can be easily checked if they do not get a chance to act on that motivation and to display their ability to learn. In a classroom with a fifty-to-one ratio of students to teacher, a youngster who wants to prove to those in the class that he or she has achieved and can recite will find it difficult. That child is not given a chance; the enthusiasm is likely to dim.

Some have expressed concern about the level of difficulty of the textbooks beginning with third grade. Some current studies show them at the right level, considering the preparation of the students and the difficulty level of the language. We are looking for clues in many directions to understand what has happened to our youngsters to cause this decline that begins at the third grade and continues.

QUESTION: Are the textbooks for third graders too hard or too easy?

COMMENT: Some have felt that they may be too difficult; I do not know that it is true.

QUESTION: If students are really doing better early on, why would some argue that textbooks are too difficult? If this evidence shows that the third graders are doing better than they were a decade ago, why should there now be a problem that third-grade textbooks are too hard; wouldn't it go the other way?

COMMENT: Teachers do not appear to use textbooks as religiously for classroom instruction as they did some time ago. Some people feel that the textbooks have made too big a jump in the level of their instruction from the

53

third grade to the fourth grade, as evidenced by the decline in learning at this point. As I indicated earlier, that is not a proven fact, only speculation.

QUESTION: Mr. Hoopes and Mr. Rhodes, do you have any general thoughts about why there should be this apparent paradox of improvement in the lower grades and decline in the high schools, and perhaps also in colleges?

COMMENT: We should not leap from the lower grades to the high schools; that's too big a jump. We can focus just on the jump from the primary grades to the fourth and fifth grades. A big decline occurs there.

COMMENT: Anything I said would be pure speculation, but one cannot rule out the impact of television on growing children and the competition of all kinds for their free time.

COMMENT: Something that occurs to me, not to answer the question directly, is that the magazine industry uses a little more than 2 million tons of paper in a year, approximately half in advertising. The book industry uses 800,000 tons of paper a year, most of which goes into book production. I think we overlook the fact that paperbacks can help people form the reading habit and that there are without doubt a great many more paperback titles published and sold now than there used to be. When the book industry is in the doldrums, business may dip because there are not as many millions of books sold in a given year; but in the long run certainly the number of books published and sold has increased vastly.

I contend that this is evidence that people are reading more and that even if they are reading some things that perhaps are not what the intellectuals might like them to read, they will form the habit of reading. I am also not especially worried about the simplification of text. My boss at the *Reader's Digest*, DeWitt Wallace, could talk and write in four and five-letter words and could communicate eloquently. He could send me something handwritten in two sentences on foolscap that told me more than many people could tell me in a page. I think there is an art to simple, direct expression. When I go over the Triborough Bridge in Manhattan and see a bunch of yellow objects, filled with sand and labeled "impact attenuater," I know that what I see is only a bumper.

COMMENT: I agree with what you said about paperbacks: They are wonderful, and they do proliferate, and they do begin people in the reading habit. "Reading Is Fundamental," founded on the distribution of paperbacks in the inner cities, has been a great success. It has given children the pleasure of owning their own books—of reading them and nurturing them—and has obviously led to their reading books again.

QUESTION: I am confused by the title of the program and the direction the program has taken to this point. I feel as if we spent the day with Gutenberg, which is fine with me because I am more comfortable there, too. We have touched only tentatively, though, upon future technology. Where are we with the words that are going to appear white on green or the funny print that spits out because the checks have to be read by machines? These are all literacy skills that we derogatorily label computer literacy. Although the personal or microcomputer is not yet in very many homes except among the well-to-do, many decisions at a very high level can be made with the aid of new technology now. One needs certain technical skills, of course, but this vast amount of information engulfing us requires skimming skills, thinking skills, and evaluation skills.

Somehow I feel as if today we have not talked about tomorrow; we have talked about the way it has been—the growth of x industry, the amount of newsprint, the number of readers, the number of subscribers, and so on. Nineteen eighty-four is right around the corner, though, and what follows that is pretty close.

DR. LEVINE: Those of us here do represent a group of people highly committed to the form of literacy that has existed to this point. It is also true that we are on the brink of a change, and that change will bring in its wake variations in the definition of literacy.

An important point made in one of the papers was a distinction between information and education. A great deal of what will be available to us through computer technology falls into the category of information, which in itself brings requirements for certain literacy skills. I see real danger in confusing those two.

We also need to differentiate between the *processes* of literacy and the *substance* of literacy, a distinction that has something to do with the information-education dichotomy.

QUESTION: In the "Reading Is Fundamental" program, one of our concerns is the availability of books at a cost low-income people can afford. We can reach quite a number of children across the country with free books, and we find that children can be turned on to reading, whatever their racial or ethnic background, the educational level of their parents, or the income level of their group. However, beyond the books that they are able to get in our program, books simply are not available to them at places where they go and at a price that they can afford. I know of only one major publisher that mass markets children's books in supermarkets, the K-Marts, and places where children are likely to be. Is the book industry giving any consideration either to production at a price that young people can afford or to distribution at places where young people are likely to be?

COMMENT: You pose a very difficult question, of course. There is nothing, naturally, that book publishers and magazine and newspaper publishers would like better than to sell more books. Whether we can in fact reduce cost to a level affordable to the average citizen of the inner city is very doubtful, however. We are plagued by the reduction in funds in all of the institutions that historically have bought books: school libraries, public libraries, and university libraries. In the near term, I do not see much salvation other than in programs such as "Reading Is Fundamental," which are, in effect, financed by local citizen groups in the various cities.

To take a highly speculative leap into the future, though, I foresee that if the process of compression goes on in the microcomputer industry, there is no reason why at some point in the future a single, large book cannot be printed on a single silicone chip. If this technique becomes commonplace, the theoretical savings in cost would be great. Forests would not have to be cut down to get the book; the book would not have to be warehoused; the wholesaler and the retailer might be eliminated. A publisher might in fact send a letter-sized envelope to a subscriber containing twelve or fifteen books. The reader would insert the chip into a reading device, which might for aesthetic purposes look like a real leather-covered book, and adjust for print size; the translating machine would translate the binary language into English. The reader would take it from there. I do not think that sort of thing is beyond the realm of possibility in the next twenty years.

COMMENT: I come to you today right out of the classroom trenches, having spent this morning in my classroom, where I teach the eighth grade. In a little hiatus from my teaching career, I went to the Associated Press with an idea that news could be consistently and daily connected to instructional material. I had had experiences with children who would not read at all suddenly being able to read when the instruction was connected with an event happening in the world. In my class, this morning, I connected virtually every instructional activity with a breaking news event out of the *Washington Post*. I have been freed by my school to use the *Washington Post* as my major textbook in class. I find that if I trace the historical antecedents of any breaking news event, those antecedents ground themselves in a multidisciplinary curriculum and frequently at many grade levels.

In my experiences, I found a great enmity between U.S. education and U.S. journalism. Journalism or the printed word did not seem to have much respect for education. The print media never perceived a real and fundamental conviction that news and education could ally themselves behind a curriculum that would serve us through the twentieth century. We have Pac-Man students. I perceive these students as fundamentally different. Their games are in the fourth dimension. Time and space are a part of their birthright; while we marvel at the space shuttle, these children expect it. Advanced technology has made a basic change in the way they perceive reality, and we simply must connect with it. When as a teacher, I connect the world of events with my demands on the students, the test scores take meteoric leaps, not because of any particular genius I have as a teacher, but because the students' instruction is as large as their view.

It has been my experience, though, that the printed medium has been at best indifferent to formal education and its goals and at worst almost hostile to alignment with formal education for such a program.

DR. REED: I am sure you would agree that there is no one methodology that works on everybody. We have to make assessment of needs and assessment of what is effective so that we bring that knowledge to bear upon the youngsters that we are faced with. The approach you have developed is absolutely sound. The more we can relate reality to what we do in the classrooms, the more effective our teaching will be. We must examine those methods of teaching that deal with the problems that we face. You have done so, but you probably would admit that the methods you are using are not necessarily effective with everybody or that they are more effective with some than with others. We have to assess and reassess constantly what we are doing and find out what approaches work and what approaches do not.

QUESTION: How do you find the *Washington Post*'s attitude to be toward connecting breaking news with instruction on a daily basis? Do you perceive that this technique is a viable approach to education?

DR. REED: Absolutely. In our "Success in Reading" program which had been relegated to elementary school in the past but has now moved into junior high school, I see teachers using the paper to relate the classroom to breaking news. The paper is delivered daily to the classroom, and teachers have a golden opportunity to use the paper as part of their curriculum. I am convinced that this program will have more of an effect this year and in years to come because the junior high schools and even the senior high schools will participate. I consider the newspaper a very effective tool in classroom instruction.

QUESTION: Dr. Reed, as a former superintendent of schools in the District of Columbia and as a former assistant secretary of the Department of Education, what suggestions would you have as to what could be done by federal, state, and local governments with respect to aliteracy?

DR. REED: Most urban school systems—that is, the boards of education and the superintendents—are grappling with the situation they find themselves in. Because we do have large numbers of youngsters not developing the necessary reading skills in prekindergarten through twelfth grade, we must

57

do what we can to turn that situation around. The Office of Education, for example, can do research, disseminate information on those programs that have been effective, and make those programs available to communities with like situations and like populations. Research is one of the main contributions the federal government can make. We do have to be careful that the federal government does not dictate to school districts what they should teach and how they should teach. From a research standpoint, however, the federal government is in the ideal position to gather information and make it available to any school district that wishes to investigate promising programs. Most school systems do not know how to deal with the problems that confront them.

MR. THIMMESCH: Mr. Rhodes, does the success of the magazine industry show that people are increasingly interested in very specialized things? Is this market trend a reflection of the "me" generation? Have the increasingly specialized magazines flourished at the expense of the general interest magazines that have declined or folded?

MR. RHODES: Yes and no. General interest magazines have not gone away. The *Reader's Digest* is certainly a general interest magazine, with more circulation than any other magazine in the country. On the topic of science, which was raised earlier, in the past three or four years, we have seen several notable science magazines started after *Scientific American* became a success: We had *Science 81*, which became *Science 82*, we have *Science Digest*, and we now have *Discover*. If the circulation of all three of these is totaled, about 2½ million copies per issue have been generated that did not exist at all three or four years ago. They all address science with much more depth than the science section of *Time Magazine*, which was where the editors of *Scientific American* first worked; *Scientific American* was an outgrowth of that.

We certainly do see specialization, of course, in magazines that, for example, deal with doctors' leisure time. Although we have all sorts of magazines—regional magazines, city magazines, magazines for particular sports, and for every imaginable thing—the fact should not be overlooked that many of the major magazines started as much as fifty, eighty, ninety, a hundred years ago—and are still very popular. *Good Housekeeping* is a classic example. People still find many useful things in *Good Housekeeping*.

DR. LEVINE: I came to this conference with the perspective of an educator, one familiar with the problems and the achievements of our schools in terms of teaching people how to read. I have some concerns about whether we are teaching children in our schools the value of reading along with the skills of reading. We have addressed an ambitious question here, and in the course of our deliberations I found the definitions of literacy, illiteracy, and aliteracy blurred together, at times indistinguishable, in the sense that one creates the other. In terms of focusing on just the question of aliteracy, which was our charge, one issue seems particularly urgent as we face the technological changes that we are, indeed, in the midst of now: the necessity of drawing a clear distinction between the mere acquisition of information and education itself.

MR. THIMMESCH: As I think over what was said and debated here today, I consider myself fortunate. I thought I had pretty well researched this topic, but I realize now how much I learned today and what there is yet to learn. We certainly know that various components of the media are quite concerned with aliteracy. I think we also defined the difference between information and knowledge. If I were to pose the question again on whether the decision-making process could be endangered by aliteracy, I would have to conclude maybe. It is up to all of us to make sure that it isn't.

SELECTED AEI PUBLICATIONS

The Private Sector in the Public School: Can It Improve Education? Marsha Levine, ed. (1985, 77 pp., $4.95)

The Higher Learning and the New Consumerism, Hanna Holborn Gray (1983, 17 pp., $3.00)

Meeting Human Needs: Toward a New Public Philosophy, Jack A. Meyer, ed. (1982, 469 pp., cloth $34.95, paper $13.95)

Debating National Education Policy: 1981-1982 High School Debate Analysis, High School Debate. (1981, 124 pp., $6.25)

Tuition Tax Credits and Alternatives, Legislative Analysis (1978, 50 pp., $3.75)

Rising Costs in Education: The Federal Response? Ernest L. Boyer, Bob Packwood, John Ryor, Thomas Sowell, John Charles Daly, mod. (1978, 44 pp., $3.75)